Farrukh Mukhtarov

Systems for ensuring national information security

AF625222

Farrukh Mukhtarov

Systems for ensuring national information security

ScienciaScripts

Imprint
Any brand names and product names mentioned in this book are subject to trademark, brand or patent protection and are trademarks or registered trademarks of their respective holders. The use of brand names, product names, common names, trade names, product descriptions etc. even without a particular marking in this work is in no way to be construed to mean that such names may be regarded as unrestricted in respect of trademark and brand protection legislation and could thus be used by anyone.

Cover image: www.ingimage.com

This book is a translation from the original published under ISBN 978-620-7-46877-5.

Publisher:
Sciencia Scripts
is a trademark of
Dodo Books Indian Ocean Ltd. and OmniScriptum S.R.L publishing group

120 High Road, East Finchley, London, N2 9ED, United Kingdom
Str. Armeneasca 28/1, office 1, Chisinau MD-2012, Republic of Moldova, Europe
Printed at: see last page
ISBN: 978-620-7-94916-8

Contents

The monograph is intended for specialists engaged in ensuring national and information security of the state, as well as for employees of diplomatic relations.

The basic concepts of ensuring national information security, models of ensuring security system, classification of information threats and characteristic of their consequences, construction of information protection system, peculiarities of organisation of information security in the strategy of interstate relations are considered.

The book is recommended for researchers engaged in the study of contemporary international relations and world politics, specialists in the field of international and national information security, as well as for a wide range of readers interested in this issue.

Reviewers:

S.F.Ergashev - Doctor of Technical Sciences, Professor;

A.M.Rasulov - Doctor of Ph.-M. sciences, Professor;

O.H.Otakulov - Candidate of Technical Sciences, Associate Professor.

PREDICTION

The problems of ensuring national information security of the Republic of Uzbekistan to a greater or lesser extent are reflected not only in the studies and theoretical developments of domestic and foreign scientists, but also in official documents. Such concepts as: "national security", "information security", "information organisation of the state" are the basis of various political doctrines and concepts of the majority of public, political organisations and movements of the country. They have become the subject of the lawmaking process and attract close attention of the mass media.

The legislative and executive authorities of the Republic of Uzbekistan, the political leadership of the country, scientists and practitioners perceive the provision of national information security as one of the most urgent and vital for the current state and prospects for the development of statehood, democracy, guarantees of protection of the interests of society and the individual. Socio-political reflection of these problems is largely determined by the dynamics of modern political processes associated with the formation of a new world order, the objective processes of changing the role and place of the Republic of Uzbekistan in the world political arena, taking place against the background of crisis phenomena in the modernisation of our state, including in the information sphere.

The issues of ensuring national information security, directly related to the reform of the information organisation of the state, find their priority reflection in the political statements of state and public figures of various levels, in the conceptual guidelines of social movements and political organisations and their leaders.

Modern scholars and practitioners consider the concept of "security" from a variety of positions. However, the most widespread approach is the approach according to which security is understood as "the state of protection of society and its components from internal and external threats, which is a property of a social system".

Along with the fact that in most spheres of the state's activity there are positive changes in the implementation of reforms, it should be emphasised that the development of the information organisation of the state is objectively going through a difficult period. As a result, the information sphere, its resources, including their protection, lag behind other institutions of modern domestic society. This circumstance negatively affects not only the information organisation of the state, but also the state of information security of the country, information security of the individual and society as a whole.

The most important role in ensuring national information security of the state is undoubtedly played by its defence, which is created by the state through a number of measures and is designed to counteract real and potential threats to national security coming from both outside and inside the country.

Of particular importance to ensuring national information security are those countries that are, or aspire to be, great powers. The governments of such states realise that without taking into account the information factor they will not be able to protect their geopolitical interests, as well as to influence the foreign policy of other countries, determine the main directions of political development of certain regions and influence world politics as a whole. This statement fully applies to the foreign policy course of such influential states, whose leadership also pays great attention to the issues of their own national information security and the development of a comprehensive system, as well as its implementation.

It is also necessary to note the need to consider the key directions of such activities and to give a general assessment of the place and role of modern Uzbekistan in the global information society, to determine the relevance of the topic of this monograph.

The scientific significance of this monograph is conditioned by the necessity of its study in our country, as the problem of formation of national information security, as well as the development of the latest methods of implementation of this task, and their adaptation to the changing conditions of modern international relations is today the most important task for specialists in the field of information security.

Teshaboev T.Z.,
Rector of Tashkent Financial Institute Doctor of Economics, Professor

INTRODUCTION

One of the important directions of ensuring sustainable development of mankind in the foreseeable future is mastering the results of the ongoing scientific and technological revolution, including the results obtained in the field of automation of processes of obtaining, transferring, storing and disseminating information, formation of the global information space. The application of modern information and communication technologies and computer equipment in the socio-economic, political and spiritual spheres of society and in the fulfilment of public administration tasks is expanding.

The potential of information and communication technologies is being actively used to improve the quality of life of citizens, to help them realise their constitutional rights and freedoms as human beings and citizens, to form civil society institutions, to increase the participation of citizens in solving their pressing problems, and to improve the effectiveness of the activities of State and local authorities.

These processes inevitably increase the dependence of individuals, organisations, state bodies and institutions on the sustainability of the functioning of the information infrastructure of society, the security of its use for the implementation of fundamental rights and freedoms, legitimate interests of citizens, the interests of society and the state. Sustainability of functioning and security of use of information infrastructure become an important factor in improving the competitiveness of the country and ensuring its national security.

Countering new challenges and threats is associated, among other things, with ensuring national information security of individuals, organisations, society and the state as a whole. It includes organisational, legal, personnel, technical, financial and other types of security. This monograph focuses on the legal and organisational provision of national information security in the strategy of interstate relations, which play a system-forming role in this counteraction. Through the efforts of the legislator, the legal support of national information security, in fact, has developed into an independent sub-branch of information law. Organisational support is an effective tool for coordinating the efforts of subjects of ensuring national information security on the most dangerous threats, stability of functioning and security of use of information infrastructure of society.

In the proposed monograph, based on the author's research and conceptual approaches, the most relevant aspects of legal support of national information security, as well as the most important aspects of its organisational support are systematically outlined.

The practical significance of this monograph lies in the fact that it considers the problems of forming a system for ensuring national information security as an orderly set of normative, organisational and technical solutions that allow not only to counter threats to national information security, but also to increase the transparency of the process of building and functioning of such systems.

The conclusions and recommendations proposed in the monograph are based on the analysis of specific normative and methodological materials, supported by illustrative illustrations and have a significant potential for further development.

The materials of the monograph will be useful for scientists and specialists dealing with the issues of ensuring national information security, as well as for students studying relevant academic courses.

In addition to the introduction, the monograph includes four chapters.

The first chapter "The current state of the influence of information technologies on the development of interstate relations" discusses such issues as system-forming concepts of information, the influence of information technologies on the development of interstate relations, trends in the development of global information space, as well as analyses the management systems of Internet resources in ensuring state security, shows the evolution of approaches to the studied problems from the point of view of the individual, society and the state.

In the second chapter "The main principles of formation of digital diplomacy in interstate relations" the main priority principles of formation of digital diplomacy are considered, the factors of threats to information resources in interstate relations are classified, and the classification of confidential information resources and objects in interstate information security is made, the methods of ensuring information security in interstate relations and ensuring the security of critical information resources are proposed.

The third chapter "Conceptual models of ensuring information security of interstate relations" is an exclusive material, where the author's approaches to the study of organisational and legal problems of formation of the system of ensuring information security of interstate relations, as well as international information security, where social aspects related to the philosophical content of the concept of "secrecy" are considered in a concentrated form, where the correlation between all types of secrets is shown.Also in this chapter, the author's approaches to the study of organisational and legal problems of formation of the system of ensuring information security of interstate relations, as well as international information security are presented.

The final fourth chapter "Methods of improving the system of ensuring information security of the state" outlines methods of creating virtual communicative information spaces of interstate relations, methods and means of constructing the image of informants and their organisational structures, and also substantiates digital diplomacy as a means of operational introduction into mass consciousness. At the same time, systematic approaches to improving interstate relations on the platforms of professional social networks are attached.

The monograph also contains a List of Recommended Literature, which may be useful in studying the relevant sections.

The presented material, collected on the pages of the monograph, allows to introduce the reader to the range of problems of ensuring national information security at the levels of the individual, society and the state, including relevant organisational and legal aspects of information protection, including state and commercial secrets.

The monograph is recommended for researchers engaged in the study of contemporary international relations and world politics, specialists in the field of international and national information security, as well as for a wide range of readers interested in this issue.

CHAPTER I

THE CURRENT STATE OF INFLUENCE OF INFORMATION TECHNOLOGIES ON DEVELOPMENT INTERSTATE RELATIONS

This chapter discusses such issues as system-forming concepts of information, the impact of information technologies on the development of interstate relations, trends in the development of global information space, as well as analyses the management systems of Internet resources in ensuring state security, shows the evolution of approaches to the studied problems from the point of view of the individual, society and the state.

§1.1 Analysing the impact of information technologies of communication networks on the development of interstate relations

Information processes in changing contemporary international relations

Information processes on a global scale, which lead to the fact that the information space is increasingly filled with political content, and in the political space, the intensity of foreign policy interactions is increasing, due to the penetration of information and communication technologies in all spheres of life of states.

Foreign policy relations go through complex cycles of development, and this is expressed in the fact that the world order is changing, there are horizontal and vertical changes in it. Vertical changes can mean a change in the status of strong and weak actors (actors) - states. This manifests itself in the weakening of the positions of states that were strong in the recent past, and in the increase of the international status of states that for a long period of time were considered developing, but did not have optimal development results.

The institutional approach has its own specificity in the study of the modernisation of international relations and should help to determine what new standards, norms, rules of foreign policy relations will be characteristic of developing countries with each other and with more developed countries with higher levels of information infrastructure development, intensity of communications, and other characteristics of information processes. Of particular interest at present are the political institutions and processes emerging and operating on the world stage with the participation of developing countries, and this participation is becoming more and more active.

When considering the development of such institutions and the possibility of forming new foreign policy relations with the participation of developing countries, we should always bear in mind that all this is taking place in the context of another complex and multilateral process - globalisation, which now covers all spheres of interaction between states and societies around the world.

Informatisation is penetrating into international relations, contributing to the formation of a new information and political space. Whichever state has a more developed information infrastructure has more opportunities to influence international relations, the domestic political situation, public consciousness and behaviour. And this applies not only to state structures, but also to such international organisations that are created in the real and interact in the virtual space.

Informatisation is becoming a means of communication that unites new emerging movements, parties, organisations and foundations that advocate opposition forces. Thanks to information technologies (IT) and the acceleration of social communications, it is possible to create out-of-state or supranational structures that represent a serious force against state power and the interference of other states.

This is why political science faces a scientific problem: to investigate the emergence of informational international relations, when international communications do not involve states with their representatives, but rapidly emerging groups, organisations with their political leaders and spread their influence across regions.

The social construction of new institutional norms, standards, codes, and the formation of new types of international relations (e.g., integration) is underway. This is facilitated by the informatisation of many societies; the increasing role of communications facilitates the formation of social ties and social capital.

Types of social processes operating in society can also be found in international relations and in the division of political forces on the world stage, as there are also established institutional norms, standards and codes. These types of social processes include: rivalry (conflict as a type of rivalry), co-operation (partnership as a type of co-operation).

In the 21st century, integration processes are intensifying, and the emerging international unions, groups, megacivilisational elements will not only defend their interests, but also introduce new rules, patterns of behaviour, principles of international relations, principles of domestic and foreign policy formation. This is facilitated by the increase in communications with the use of new information

technologies.
The changing polarisation of the world has created the basis for new types of international relations, which can be rightly called "megacivilisational". The African Union's activities and those of NEPAD, which mainly take into account the economic, social and political problems common to developing countries, can be called such a basis.
The deepening of integration processes and the development of institutional structures can be traced back to the EU in Europe. A certain moving balance is emerging, and the intertwining of the three levels - supranational, national, regional - is becoming more and more differentiated. For example:
- the principle of subsidiarity introduced in the EU treaty framework;
- Establishment of a new institution - the Committee of the Regions - as a deliberative body (composed of representatives of regional and local communities);
- the practice of representing the nation-state by regions of federal states.
Information processes are peculiar accelerators of foreign policy changes. The foundations for such changes were laid in the second half of the 20th century. It is possible that a number of developing countries will not only come to the forefront, but also form a new integrated structure. The drivers of such change vary from State to State. For some countries of South and South-East Asia (India, China, Malaysia) it is significant economic and technical progress, for some Latin American countries (Argentina, Brazil, Venezuela, Chile) - significant changes in domestic politics. A redistribution around the advanced developing countries and a redistribution of the statuses of these countries themselves may begin in the near future.
Already in 1989, the Arab Maghreb Union was formed in North Africa, involving Algeria, Libya, Mauritania, Morocco and Tunisia. But the North African region represents five closed markets. Significant differences between these countries and the rest of the African continent can be seen even when comparing GDP and personal income. In information infrastructure, there are also profound differences between the named groups of countries.
Integration represents an alternative development path for developing countries, a way to achieve self-reliant progress. The successful

process of such integration requires more mature socio-economic relations, developed market mechanisms, and new institutional forms of foreign policy.

In our opinion, the formation of such forms will occur primarily in the sphere of information security in developing countries. It is information security that is becoming a mandatory norm of modern international relations, but so far it has not been formalised as a requirement, but rather as a need expressed at the international level. Now this norm is mostly unregulated. And due to the strengthening of mass communications, on the basis of politicisation of the information space, it becomes necessary and possible to develop such institutional norms, which will not only contribute to the development of NMIP, but also to the regulation of modern international relations.

The increasing use of information technology is dramatically changing the daily lives of millions of people. They bring changes not only in the internal politics of the most diverse countries of the world in terms of development, but also in the relations between these countries, in the role played in the world system by international organisations, social movements, financial groups, criminal organisations and individuals. The very subject of the theory of international relations is changing. Theoretical understanding of modern international relations without taking into account the role of new information technologies becomes simply impossible. Such qualitative changes are reflected in the process of making foreign policy decisions. Nowadays, an analyst working with specific foreign policy problems faces the consequences of the information revolution not only when studying this or that phenomenon of international life.

Information technologies are changing the very labour of the international researcher. Recognising the nature of these changes is a prerequisite for solving almost any applied problem.

To investigate the role of information technology in contemporary international relations. In order to achieve such a goal, two main tasks need to be accomplished. First, the impact of new information technologies on contemporary international relations (including changes in the role of the state in international relations and changes in the forms of international conflict) should be examined. Secondly, a clear understanding of the changes that new information technologies bring to the study of international relations is required.

Nowadays, information is largely the product of data collected by electronic sensors. Electronic communications have expanded the area in which information can be exchanged in a timely manner. Data processing software and hardware are also developing rapidly.

The Internet has created an unprecedented need for constant and rapid exchange of information in the military, government and private sectors. Information networks connected to the Internet are constantly processing private, business and military information. Such qualitative changes in the processes of data collection, its processing into information and dissemination of this information form the basis of the so-called information revolution.

Information is now a strategic resource that must be managed effectively in order to achieve superiority. Because information plays such a key role, any action taken in the information domain can have consequences for the physical domain (materials, personnel, finances) and for the abstract domain (belief system).

Information Age technologies make the battlefield environment more dynamic and unpredictable. This makes national economies more sensitive to global developments, raises the cultural and political consciousness of parts of the world's population, and fuels radical movements that push for global fragmentation and destabilisation. Information Age technologies can present the results of military actions (small or large) to a global audience almost immediately. Images of war and peace - real or created - can influence national will and public opinion even before audiences verify their authenticity. Paradoxically, the real-time flow of information imposes an even greater need for intelligence gathering.

The information revolution is changing the face of institutions. It eliminates hierarchies, disperses and redistributes power (often towards smaller elements), crosses and redraws boundaries, and expands the horizons of time and space. The information revolution reinforces the importance of networks (e.g. social or communication networks). It enables different and remote actors to communicate, consult, coordinate with each other over greater distances and with better information than before. The information revolution will be the cause of shifts in the ways of conflict between societies and the methods of warfare - conflict at the societal level and warfare in command and control at the military level. Both types are related to information, they are also just forms of warfare over the knowledge of society or the military about itself and its adversaries.

Information technology is the "great equaliser" for states, both in times of peace and war. This technology knows no national boundaries and is spreading all over the world. Many components and systems are available on the international market. The information revolution has created an environment in which state sovereignty is being redefined. Conflict between states and non-state associations is therefore as likely as conflict between two states.
The history of wars can be divided into three major periods (or waves) corresponding to the history of development of human civilisations: agrarian, industrial and informational. Future wars for civilisations of the third wave should take the form of information warfare. It is often thought that information warfare is a war based on perfect communication systems, access to space, and real-time decision-making.
Since ancient times, enemies have fought wars in five dimensions-political, social, technological, operational, and supply-which are linked to the four elements of national power-political, social-psychological, military, and economic. Ignoring even one of these can lead to catastrophic defeat. The political dimension consists of political goals and politics as a process. Political objectives have always guided wars, although not always in a completely consistent manner. The social dimension-the attitudes and commitments of people-also remains important. Technology affects every dimension and all levels of warfare. It interacts with culture and events across time and space and influences the duration, nature and outcomes of conflict. The operational dimension relates to the conduct of war. It consists mainly of attempts to dominate the battlefield and break the enemy's will to fight.
The last dominant operational concept of the pre-information era was the concept of sequential operations, when more and more reserves were gradually (by echelons) introduced into the battle, and victory depended on the availability of these reserves and the correct choice of the moment for their use.
We see that the revolution in warfare has made it necessary to consider the information dimension as well. However, we should not consider information as a physical dimension (like territory, air or sea). Information superiority does not work in the same way as air superiority. Fighting under new conditions requires a completely new paradigm. Its main points can be summarised as follows:

- each component of the system plays a role in determining the outcome;
- Predictable and unpredictable phenomena coexist and interact, leading to complex networks with a huge number of variables, making it impossible to predict the outcome;
- a small change in the input system can lead to disproportionately large changes in outcomes;
- systems - individuals, armies, bureaucracies - tend to evolve towards their own increasing complexity;
- complex systems can reorganise themselves when faced with challenges.

Rivalries (or hostilities) within such a paradigm are most likely to take the form of information warfare, which refers to a conflict involving information at the strategic level between states or societies. It can be directed at public or elite attention. It can include diplomacy, propaganda and psychological campaigns, political and cultural subversion, introducing false data into local media, penetrating information networks and databases, and promoting opposition or dissident movements through computer networks. The main targets are those societal and economic areas that are relatively easy to access.

Therefore, the consideration of the impact of information and communication technologies on modern international relations and political processes is relevant from both theoretical and practical points of view. Information and communication technologies significantly change social relations. New technologies transform the purpose and functions of public and international institutions - states, financial groups, political parties and international organisations. Theoretical consideration of international relations outside the context of information and communication technologies can no longer be sufficient for objective and comprehensive reflection. Absolutely all areas of international relations are undergoing qualitative changes: from the process of developing foreign policy decisions to international conflicts. Understanding the nature of the development of political processes under the influence of information and communication technologies is an important prerequisite for solving any applied problem in the sphere of international relations.

The range of information abuse is quite large and it can be not only about unauthorised information, "spam", creation of illegal websites, but also about serious crimes committed out of national or religious hatred. It is no secret that the Internet has become a "safe haven" for terrorist organisations, including international ones, which are engaged in active "information warfare" with the state and society all over the world. It should be taken into account that, having a sign of globality (beyond territoriality) and being a cheap means of communication, the Internet often becomes a "place" for committing various kinds of offences.

Information technologies provide equal opportunities both to conduct negative policies and to develop ways to prevent them and even to improve the methods of conducting effective foreign policy. At the same time, it is necessary to fight against information abuses with adequate information methods.

Technical features and consumer capabilities of information technologies make it possible to re-evaluate at the political level many stereotypes that have developed in the international way of life, forcing states to take a new approach to the choice of foreign policy guidelines and ways of resolving political conflicts. One of the ways of conducting negative policy is information wars. Information methods of international confrontation, being less burdensome and costly from the economic point of view, are beginning to gradually supplant traditional means of force. Information becomes both a powerful weapon and a vulnerable target for the enemy. Against the background of intensive integration of citizens and organisations into international relations, as well as due to the availability of information weapons to a wide range of persons, a problem arises in distinguishing military actions from crimes (including terrorism).

The Internet in international politics has grown significantly. Today, the Internet is a comprehensive tool of political influence and impact on socio-economic development in the context of globalisation of international relations.

The Internet is one of the factors in the development of democracy in the world. It is with its help that non-state actors, including non-governmental organisations and citizens, can expand the spheres of their participation in international and domestic activities. In fact, the Internet is becoming an important indicator of civil rights and freedoms in various countries of the world. This is confirmed by regular reviews by international organisations such as Amnesty International, Human Rights Watch and Reporters Without Borders.

Thus, another important conclusion from the paper is that the development of the Internet has led to an increase in the influence of non-state actors on the world stage, i.e. the influence of public institutions and individuals on politics and international relations has increased significantly.

Global information warfare differs from computer crime in that it involves hostile action by an adversary - whether an individual, a rival organisation or a hostile state - in a struggle for hegemony in the market or political arena. However, information warfare is broader than just the military dimension. It is much broader than command and control warfare. Basically the set of targets for information warfare will not be the set of military targets. "Information warfare is electronic conflict in which information is a strategic asset worthy of conquest or destruction. Computers and other communications and information systems will be first-strike targets and at the same time weapons in the new war."

In a broad perspective, information warfare is waged in many dimensions. It is a state strategy that uses all levers of national power to create advantages at the strategic level. It is more than the application of information technology to increase the effectiveness of modern instruments of warfare. It represents the actions necessary to paralyse not only the enemy's military command and control systems, but also its political and financial systems.

The quantity, technical level and accessibility of information resources already determine the level of a country's development and its status in the world community and has undoubtedly become a decisive indicator of this status.

The development of the process of informatisation of the world community generates a whole set of negative geopolitical consequences.

ICTs are rapidly becoming an important stimulus for the development of countries' military capabilities by increasing their information endowment. It becomes possible for scientifically and technologically advanced countries to use information potential to suppress and subjugate less developed and, consequently, weaker states. This inevitably leads to the accelerated polarisation of the world, which becomes a source of instability, a basis for the emergence and development of real and potential conflicts, including those that may become global in nature. Changing global and regional balances of power, increasing tensions between traditional and emerging centres of power, and the emergence of new frontiers of global confrontation give rise to the possibility of military conflicts.

Computers are fundamentally changing the very principles of warfare because they can enable more rapid and less bloody military operations. Instead of risking the loss of expensive and time-consuming military equipment and numerous troops, commanders can use computer terminals to penetrate the computer networks of foreign countries, disable radars, electronic equipment, disrupt telephone communications, i.e., affect critical infrastructure and purposefully influence the consciousness of citizens.

The vulnerability of cyberspace makes it a very attractive means for terrorist organisations, criminal groups and individual perpetrators to commit criminal acts against public interests, the security of States, organisations and citizens.

The incorporation of the latest information and telecommunications technologies and tools into the arsenals of terrorist organisations is extremely dangerous, as it radically transforms the very methods of terrorist activity. The widespread use of ICTs by extremist elements allows them to form highly effective and flexible networked organisational structures that unite disparate groups into transnational terrorist communities whose existence is very difficult to detect until the moment of a terrorist act. ICTs enable terrorist organisations to move from "pinpoint" attacks to systematic and often disguised attacks on information infrastructures. They enable even amateur hackers to use "hacking" techniques for criminal and terrorist purposes, such as the Helkern virus attack mentioned above.

Analysis of the cyber attacks that have become known shows that ICTs have already been mastered by international terrorist and extremist organisations (Hamaz, Al-Qaeda) and national separatist movements (Liberation Tigers of Tamil Eelam, etc.).

In the most general form, information weapons can be defined as technical and other means, technologies, methods and information designed to exert a "forceful" impact on the enemy's information space, defence, management, political, social, economic and other critical systems of the state in order to damage them and achieve superiority in the information confrontation.

§ 1.2 Specific features of the development of the information society and ensuring information security

Information security of a country is understood as the state of protection of its national interests in the information sphere, determined by the totality of balanced interests of an individual, society and the state.

Of the external threats to information security in the sphere of foreign policy, the greatest danger is posed by:

- information impact of foreign political, economic, military and information structures on the development and implementation of foreign policy strategy;
- The dissemination of foreign policy misinformation abroad;
- violation of the rights of domestic citizens and legal entities in the information sphere abroad;
- attempts of unauthorised access to information and impact on information resources, information infrastructure of executive authorities implementing foreign policy, representations and organisations abroad, representations to international organisations.

The term "information society" was coined by Y. Hayashi, professor at the Tokyo Institute of Technology. Researchers and developers of the theory of information society are also: M. Castells, F. Webster, E. Giddens, J. Habermas, D. Martin, G. Molitor, E. Toffler, D. Bell, Z. Brzezinski, A. King, D. Nesbit, A. Touraine, P. Drucker, M. McLuhan and others.

The information society will change the way of life, the system of values of individuals and social groups, and the importance of information values in relation to material values will increase. T. Stonier noted that transactions over material things lead to competition, while information exchange between individuals and social groups leads to co-operation. In the conditions of information society formation, individuals and social groups will have to rethink their life position, the redistribution of life values that is taking place.

The determining factor of social differentiation of the information society is the level of knowledge rather than property. The determining factor in the social differentiation of the information society is the level of knowledge, not property E. Toffler notes that in the conditions of information society formation there will be "radical changes in the sphere of production, which will inevitably entail breathtaking social changes".

In modern society, information security is the most important component of national security.

This provision is due to a number of circumstances:
At the present stage, the implementation of vital interests of an individual, society and the state is carried out through the processes of informatisation, i.e. these subjects see the implementation of their interests through the prism of receiving benefits offered by the development of information relations, and wish to develop in this direction;
The information sphere has acquired the status of a system-forming sphere and the level of economic, social and political development of society and the state largely depends on it;
the specifics of the information sphere are such that the negative consequences of the implementation of threats to information security are manifested in other spheres of life of an individual, society and the state and affect national security in political, economic and other spheres.
Analysis of existing challenges and threats in the CIS member states shows that in modern conditions the danger of committing crimes, crisis situations and other illegal actions using modern information technologies is increasing.
И. Wallerstein assumes that in 20002025 there will be a new and very significant expansion of the microeconomy on the basis of new monopolised leading industries. Such a system, in his opinion, will have the following features:
1. It will be a bipolar rather than unipolar microsystem.
2. The existing outflow of capital, mostly from the south, is rather continuing in the coming period, but the economic needs of the south are increasing rather than decreasing.
3. A demographic gap parallel to (and even exceeding) the economic gap between north and south has been created. There may be massive pressure of migration from south to north.
4. There will be no decolonisation of developing countries between 2000 and 2025, but the economic situation of the middle classes in these countries is likely to deteriorate.
5. There is an increasing tendency for liberalism to fail and for the dangerous classes to become dangerous again.
The characteristic features of information weapons include their universality, radical impact, and accessibility. It does not require large expenditures of financial resources for its activation, which makes information warfare an economical and therefore very dangerous

means of armed struggle. Its use is impersonal and can be easily disguised as peaceful activity. At the same time, it is difficult to determine its nationality and the state that carried out the information attack. The matter is further complicated by the fact that aggressions are often carried out from the territory of third countries. Information weapons do not know geographical distances and undermine the traditional concept of state borders, making them technologically permeable. The use of these weapons can take place covertly, without a declaration of war, and does not require much visible preparation. Sometimes the victim may not even realise that he or she is under information influence. In addition, due to the lack of systems and techniques that assess the threat and warn of an impending attack in advance, the possibility of countering such aggression is complicated. The development of criteria for determining the fact of an attack on information infrastructures and the creation of an "early warning system" similar to the military attack warning system created during the Cold War is difficult due to the constant and rapid evolution of the nature of threats in the infosphere.

Information weapons include means of high-precision recognition and location of equipment emitting in the radio magnetic spectrum, targeting and fire defeat; means of disabling components of radio electronic systems and software; means of disorganising the functioning of information exchange subsystems by affecting the medium and algorithm of signal propagation; means of perception management, propaganda, disinformation and, finally, psychotronic weapons.

The most dangerous is the use of information weapons against military and civilian facilities and structures that must be in a state of continuous operability and function in real time. The results of a hostile impact on their work can be catastrophic.

The problem of ensuring international information security is complicated primarily by the fact that it has not yet become an object of regulation of international law. In the era of globalisation, which has affected both the scientific-technical and information-telecommunications spheres and, to a large extent, was caused by the emergence of breakthrough developments in these areas, communications between countries are becoming increasingly dependent on information technology-based infrastructures that cross national borders. The international nature of the threats of information aggression and crime determines the need for cooperation at both the regional and global levels in order to take concerted action to reduce existing threats. No State can achieve this alone.

Awareness of the fact that the emergence and proliferation of information weapons and the militarisation of information technologies will be a powerful destabilising factor in international relations and will seriously test the entire system of international agreements on maintaining strategic stability.

The concept of information security today is reflected in the documents on international information security in the formulation: "Information security is the state of protection of individuals, society and the state and their interests from threats, destructive and other negative impacts in the information space". In this formulation, this basic concept covers the threats of socio-humanitarian nature that are becoming more and more relevant and dangerous today, in particular, the threats of dissemination of information harmful to socio-political and socio-economic systems, spiritual, moral and cultural environment of the state.

§1.3 Internet resources and trends in the development of the global information space

The development of the modern system of international relations is increasingly determined by the factor of global information space. It seems that the development of information technologies in the second half of the twentieth century was significantly accelerated by the processes of globalisation, which played a significant role in the formation of the system of international relations.

The Internet has become the basis of the global information space - a technological infrastructure that has allowed users of all countries to be united into a single information network.

Developed countries of the modern world actively use various Internet technologies to fulfil their functions. In a general sense, this trend has been called "e-government". The formation of information space, the spread of the Internet and other information technologies open up almost unlimited opportunities for transnational interaction. On a global scale, the so-called non-state actors of world politics are becoming increasingly important, whose interaction in the information space largely determines the direction of development of the entire system of international relations as a whole.

The rapid development of the Internet in recent years, on the one hand, opens up unlimited opportunities for transnational exchange of information, but, on the other hand, often does not allow the application of the norms of national legislation in relation to information resources.

It seems that the development of information technology has had a great impact on the processes of competition. In conditions of "universal awareness", on the one hand, great opportunities for unfair competition - industrial espionage, economic intelligence, theft of production secrets and other trade secrets - are opening up. On the other hand, information advantage opens up unlimited opportunities to maintain competitiveness and attract customers.

Prominent scientists V.S. Pirumov, V.D. Popov, G.G. Pocheptsov, G.V. Grachev, I.K. Melnik, S.A. Modestov, S. Datsyuk, V.A. Kopylov, V.G. Krysko, L. Malkov, V.G. Mashlykin, M.I. Abdurakhmanov, V.A. Barishpolets, V.L. Manilov, S.P. Rastorguev, S. Parinov, S.E. Zuev, V.B. Veprintsev.

The information space, or infosphere, is a very specific environment. The content of such processes as interaction in the process of joint activity, competition (through changes in the content and nature of competition between the subjects operating in the information space) is changing significantly. In terms of power confrontation, armed struggle and information confrontation, which overlaps with it but does not coincide completely, are changing.

The nature of geopolitical competition changes especially significantly in the information space due to the struggle for achieving information superiority, for possessing a more developed information resource, which opens up better opportunities to control the information resource of the enemy.

Information policy considers mainly the information-psychological component of information processes. Accordingly, the information-psychological component of the information space - the information-psychological sphere - is of the greatest importance for information policy.

The information-psychological sphere is a part of the information sphere, which is related to the effects of information on human mental activity.

It is formed by the aggregate:

- people;
- the information they exchange and perceive;

- social relations arising in connection with information exchange and information impacts on the human psyche.

Mental activity of people forms the basis for the development of all spheres of social life, determines the intellectual potential of society, its ability to develop, dignified existence in the world community. Culture, public consciousness, public opinion on all socially important events are formed on the basis of this activity. Mental activity, based on the collection, processing, storage, transmission and dissemination of information, determines the personal uniqueness of a person, his spiritual needs, motivation of behaviour, moral values, worldview, attitude to others and society as a whole.

The information sphere is a system-forming factor in the life of society. It actively influences the state of economic, political, defence and other components of national security.

In the information space there are no usual borders and territories. Distances, geography, borders can be referred to abstract artificial categories that have almost no impact on relations between individuals and entire organisations. The significance in the information space for the information policy are those of its components and processes, the impact on which by means and methods of information policy allows influencing the prospects, influencing decision-makers, controlling the systems of collection, processing, storage and transmission of information, and multiplying resources.

The main properties of the information space are as follows.

1. Information space is basic for the concepts of information warfare and information weapons. Information warfare can be defined as unauthorised activity in someone else's information space.
2. The information space is dynamic. There is no such thing as a completed state in it. Physical objects, as a rule, have strictly defined physical limits. Hence, the following consequence is possible: it is quite difficult to achieve permanent information dominance, although it is possible to achieve temporary information superiority.
3. Information space is structured. It is heterogeneous, it has attractors that attract attention and barriers that repel the consumer's attention from a given point of the information space.
4. Information space is always protected; there are places in it that are consciously defended against the entry of others. Protection simultaneously implies the presence of weaknesses and serves as their detector.

5. The information space is universal: any field of human activity relies on it. Hence the unique opportunities for impact in any professional field.
6. Information space is not directly connected to real space because of its partly intangible nature, and the ability to utilise civilian information infrastructures that reach anywhere in the world, whereas familiar military methods require their own means.
7. The information space has nationally specific ways of constructing, processing and disseminating information.

The structure of information space is a set of stable relations and connections between the elements of the system. The structure includes the general organisation of the system (subject, process, phenomenon), spatial and temporal arrangement of the system's constituent parts, etc. The structure is formed not by any connections and relations, but first of all by regular, essential ones. The most important connections and relations are called integrating; they influence other regular connections, causing the general specificity of structures within the system.

The main structural components of the information space in its synergetic representation are information fields and information flows.

Online community is a community of subjects of activity based on the mass transfer of information activity and interactions of people, groups and organisations online. The development of the Internet is accompanied by the mass transfer of people's information activity, as well as information interactions with each other, from the environment created by traditional information and communication technologies to the virtual environment of the Internet, i.e. online. Thus, one of the main results of socio-economic applications of Internet technologies is the emergence of a large number of online communities in society.

Online communities in the simplest case are groups of people whose communication is based on the use of Internet technologies (WEB-forums, mailing lists, chat rooms, etc.). In more complex cases - in addition to the virtual way of communication, people use special methods of coordination and harmonisation of their activities, which differ from both market and hierarchical models of management of socio-economic systems.

The relative simplicity of the conditions under which subjects of geopolitical competition unite into virtual coalitions in the information space is explained both by the high intensity of the emergence and development of information and information-psychological processes, and by the high ability of a virtual coalition, consisting of any number of heterogeneous subjects of geopolitical competition, to adapt to changes in the internal and external geopolitical situation, manoeuvre forces and means, and quickly restore the geopolitical situation.

The information space, due to its transgranularity and virtual nature, acts in the modern world as one of the main spheres of integration of the human community on a planetary scale.

While the benefits of the Internet are undoubtedly prevalent, the world is also confronted daily with the negative aspects of this phenomenon. We are talking primarily about such activities on the Internet as the distribution of obscene materials that threaten the moral foundations of society, in particular child pornography, neo-Nazi materials, and the use of the Internet for gambling, betting, and lotteries of all kinds in order to take money from the population.

There is little doubt that the widespread posting of pornographic "pictures" on websites significantly undermines established standards of morality in society, given that servers with such information are often visited by children and adolescents. The practice of posting pornographic photos/videos and related information on certain websites continues to gain momentum, as the Internet as a whole is currently owned by no one in particular, and therefore there is no administrative authority that could globally prohibit this practice or at least regulate it in any way.

In addition, the Internet can also serve as a means of disseminating propaganda material from criminal organisations, recipes for the manufacture of explosives and poisonous substances, weapons, narcotic and psychotropic drugs, and methods of opening electronic and other ciphers. Such information can easily be disguised, for example, as scientific and technical information.

At the same time, there are fundamentally new real threats of using the achievements in the field of new information and communication technologies for purposes incompatible with the basic principles of maintaining world stability and security, such as the sovereign equality of States, non-interference in internal affairs and the peaceful settlement of disputes and conflicts. In particular, developed countries are tempted to use their advantages in computer technology and means of information and psychological influence on individual and public consciousness for information, political, economic and cultural

expansion.
Targeted information influence on the enemy has long-standing roots. However, today, thanks to new technologies, the consequences of information impact can be comparable to the results of combat operations within the framework of traditional military confrontation. In this connection, it seems necessary to speak of information confrontation, first of all, in the context of interstate relations, as well as in relation to various terrorist and criminal organisations whose actions affect vital interests or are directly directed against one or another state. This state of affairs has put the issues of national, regional and international information security on the agenda of modern international relations. The main concepts in this area are defined by specialists as follows:
information confrontation - a form of interstate rivalry implemented by means of information influence on the management systems of other states and their armed forces, as well as on the political and military leadership and society in general, information infrastructure and mass media of these states in order to achieve beneficial goals for themselves while protecting their own information space from similar actions;
information impact - the act of using information weapons;
Information weapon - a set of technical and other means, methods and technologies designed to:
- establishing control over the information resources of a potential adversary;
- interference in the operation of its management systems and information networks, communication systems, etc. in order to disrupt their performance, up to and including complete disabling, removal, distortion of the data contained therein, or directed introduction of special information, dissemination of favourable information and disinformation in the system of public opinion formation and decision-making;
information security is a state of protection of information space, which ensures its formation and development in the interests of citizens, organisations and the state as a whole; a state of information infrastructure of the state, in which information is used strictly for its intended purpose and does not have a negative impact on information or other systems, both the state itself and other countries when using it.

Today we can say with full confidence that information security issues have become a serious problem in the development of the global information society against the background of the continuing high level of conflict in international relations.

This state of affairs led to a forced change in the direction of political thought. The political elite felt the need to plan for the upcoming development of new information and telecommunication technologies, which, due to their peculiarities, can have both positive and negative effects on society both within a particular country and within the international system. In particular, it is important to prevent the expansion of confrontation and confrontation in the information environment and the further aggravation of the "digital divide" between developed countries and the rest of the world. And such threats are, admittedly, real.

It is the state in the process of information society formation that should play the role of coordinator of the activities of various actors of society and promote the integration of citizens into the global information society with a targeted policy, while defending its interests in the global information space.

§1.4 Internet resource management systems for state security

The first decade of the XXI century witnessed cardinal transformations in the field of political communication, which is directly reflected in the intensification of social and political ties, in the shift of the power hierarchy towards decentralised network structures.

In turn, positive trends can be emphasised: ICTs open the doors for multilateral communication, including feedback possibilities, which entails the widespread use of the latter in the political process; on the Internet, the application of communication channels is non-linear (branched), which makes the factor of manipulative influence by the state much more complicated and expensive, i.e. the state is no longer able to exert maximum influence at minimum cost; the Internet assimilates all the advantages of traditional mass media, and provides users with the

As negative aspects, we note that the Internet space is strictly differentiated. All kinds of social groups, which are carriers of information, are included in computer-mediated interaction with each other, forming a single space. The structure of the Internet space contains, along with areas with high indicators of social and political interaction, areas with low activity. The areas with low activity are characterised mainly by unidirectional communication, i.e. the individual is only a recipient. This heterogeneous distribution of political activity on the Web complicates the study of political Internet communication. For example, interaction on the Web is ranked based on the degree to which Internet users are aware of political information. Traditional criteria for determining social status are being devalued: age, ethnicity, and socio-personal characteristics no longer play a key role.

The penetration of the Internet into social and political spheres of society is becoming more and more obvious as the total application of the latest Internet technologies in the system "power-society", which in turn reveals a steady tendency of power to expand the forms and methods of influence and impact on the political system and the process of formation of political decisions. Changes in the ways and forms of political communication are a kind of indicators that can be used to judge the state of the power-management process, its intensity and controllability.

There is a pressing need to ensure national security, which is dictated by the existence of real threats at different levels, namely: threats at the level of the individual - to his or her rights and freedoms; threats at the level of society - to its democratic socio-political institutions; and at the State level - threats to the independence and integrity of the State.

"National security is the state of protection of the individual, society and the state from internal and external threats, which allows to ensure constitutional rights, freedoms, decent quality and standard of living of citizens, sovereignty, territorial integrity and sustainable development, defence and security of the state".

In particular, the conceptual apparatus of the National Security Strategy, among other important components, contains the component "means of ensuring national security" - Internet, software, telecommunication technologies, including information means used in the process of ensuring national security for the purpose of collecting, forming, processing, transmitting or receiving information on the state of national security and measures to strengthen it.

The integration of Internet resources into the sphere of public administration, the intensity of e-government development due to the active adoption of various regional programmes for building an information society should increase. Therefore, the solution to the problem of ensuring national security in e-government, on the one hand, should increase the social trust of citizens in the implementation of public services provided by public administration through Internet resources; on the other hand, to ensure the protection of public e-government from threats to national security of the country.

CONCLUSIONS TO CHAPTER I

In this chapter:

- The concept and content of the institutional approach to the study of modern foreign policy relations is given. The theoretical approaches are compared, the possibilities of transformation of foreign policy relations in the conditions of informatisation are investigated;
- The impact of information technologies of communication networks on the development of interstate relations was analysed;
- specific features of information society development and information security are considered;
- Internet resources and trends in the development of the global information space are highlighted on an accessible scale;
- dictated by Internet resource management systems in ensuring state security.

CHAPTER II

BASIC PRINCIPLES OF DIGITAL DIPLOMACY IN INTERSTATE RELATIONS

In this chapter, "Basic Principles of Forming Digital Diplomacy in Interstate Relations," the main priority principles of forming digital diplomacy are considered, the factors of threats to information resources in interstate relations are classified, and a classification of confidential information resources and objects in interstate information security is made, methods of ensuring information security in interstate relations and ensuring the security of critical information resources and objects in interstate information security are proposed.

§2.1 Key Priority Principles of Digital Diplomacy Formation

In the period of formation of a new international information order and globalisation processes in the world, the words uttered almost four centuries ago by the famous English philosopher Francis Bacon, "he who owns information owns the world", acquire a qualitatively new meaning. We are not only passive witnesses, but often active participants in the process of formation and development of the market of information and knowledge as factors of production, in addition to the traditional markets of natural resources. Today we can say with full confidence that knowledge and information are becoming one of the strategic resources of the state and society, a resource of socio-economic, technological and cultural development.

Today's realities show that a country's status is increasingly determined by its capacity for development, and that capacity, in turn, is determined by the country's ability to build up and manage its information resources. Knowledge and technology influence the lives of millions of people around the world through the products, goods, services and culture they consume.

The infrastructure of information resource has very peculiar spatial and temporal characteristics, which are not limited to the national territory. Information influence is seen as a new highly effective type of weapon, often no less effective than traditional weapons and military equipment. And in the struggle for spheres of economic and political influence, developed countries are increasingly shifting the emphasis from the use of military force to the use of covert and flexible forms of struggle, one of which is the control and management of information resources of other states.

The network is more actively involved in shaping unfamiliar norms of conduct on the international stage. Progress in information technology and the accelerated growth of the role of cyberspace and social networks are creating a new reality not only for organisations and citizens, but also for states.

The content of information in social networks is beyond the control of the state, unlike television or radio. Therefore, today we are obliged to work with this channel of communication if we want to avoid large-scale distortion of information about our work.

Social media have fundamentally changed the rules of public diplomacy. In the past, the scale of influence of a competent diplomat could reach hundreds of thousands of people. Only a few could get the attention of hundreds of thousands or millions of people through radio, television or print media. However, such activity of diplomats could be in conflict with the state interests, as the state usually tries to prevent leaks of official information about the activities of the diplomatic service.

Digital diplomacy is one of the freshest techniques of the technological revolution, which is driven by the advent of networked technologies and the digitisation of almost all data.

Digital is becoming the primary form factor of information. Diplomats' creation of vast amounts of digital information and networking technologies now make it possible to utilise information previously isolated on paper, on shelves, in filing cabinets. Not only is diplomatic information being pooled, but also the knowledge of individual officers around the world is being pooled.

Interaction in professional social networks can also be useful for another tool of digital diplomacy - crowdsourcing.

Nowadays, openness is an objective necessity for the state, which operates in the information space on an equal footing with other actors and sources of information. Digital diplomacy is designed to promptly provide adequate information, refute incorrect information, and confirm information from official sources. However, this often entails certain risks.

The experience and information accumulated by various departments of the foreign policy structure of a state, thanks to modern ICTs, can be successfully used in different parts of the globe, regardless of the location of the source and consumer.

Digital diplomacy is mainly of an applied nature and is particularly useful in working with foreign audiences, broadcasting official positions and shaping the image of the state.

Digital diplomacy has the power to explain why a decision was made, what results it will lead to, how it will affect the foreign policy process, i.e. to open access to the results of traditional diplomacy to the general public.

For foreign policy agencies, the time for digital diplomacy has long since arrived. They have only to make a choice: to passively observe the changes taking place and remain aloof from technological progress or to accept this reality and with it master the opportunities and advantages that digital diplomacy offers.

In some cases, a diplomat's direct communication with the public may be effective (for example, when it is part of his/her direct functions as an official representative), while in other cases it may be perceived negatively. In general, a skilful combination of official and public aspects of activity gives undoubted advantages in influencing foreign states and societies. The variants of such combinations can be very diverse, and in all cases the state co-operates with civil society organisations of both its own country and international partners in order to exert external influence.

Diplomatic structures actively use modern communication channels to influence the society of foreign countries. First of all, it is the Internet, social networks, blogs - what has come to be known as "new media".

Social media - Facebook, Twitter or the video hosting site Youtube - are increasingly becoming tools for ordinary people, their users, to influence international politics.

In addition, the changed global political landscape (primarily the economic interdependence of countries due to globalisation) makes it necessary for states to take more active foreign policy actions to strengthen their own "soft power". In addition, the changed world political landscape (first of all, the economic interdependence of countries due to globalisation) actualises the need for more active foreign policy actions on the part of states to strengthen their own "soft power" in conditions where the use of military or economic coercive measures looks doubtful. In this regard, "public diplomacy 2.0", one of the tasks of which is precisely the formation of a positive image of the state abroad, can be considered as an extremely useful tool of foreign policy activity. Also, this direction of public diplomacy can be used to discredit geopolitical competitors in the international arena or as a means of promoting the articulation of one's own position on a wide range of issues on the current agenda in the conditions of "information wars".

One of the most important subjects of "public diplomacy 2.0" (and in some countries the key one) is mass media oriented towards foreign audiences: TV channels, radio broadcasting companies, news agencies, print media with accounts on social networks, microblogs, and video hosting sites. Their work is especially noticeable in periods of aggravation of the international situation, when they are not only a tool for articulating the state's position on a number of issues on the current agenda, but also the main tool in the "ideological" confrontation with competitors.

The rapid development of electronic media and communication has created an opportunity for the active and rapid introduction of myths and values into the mass consciousness in order to both disorient the population and shape its desired perceptions.

The emerging information environment is beginning to dictate its own rules of the game to state bodies engaged in foreign policy. It complicates the international system, expands the list of its participants, changes the formats of socio-political events directly affecting the world configuration, and becomes a factor of instability and the emergence of additional threats. It is not only about the information component, but also about the patterns of formation and course of conflicts and other significant processes.

Information threat is considered as one of the most important threats to the national security of the country. The Internet is perceived as a channel for spreading extremism and terrorism, imposing alien ideology and foreign policy propaganda, as a means of information warfare. However, ensuring information security does not exclude the use of the Internet as a means of realising internal and external goals of the state. The consequences of the spread of the Internet are multifaceted and are not exhausted by security issues.

In any case, the Internet space has entered a new stage of its development, when the problem of control over it becomes the subject of an increasingly fierce struggle. Moreover, we can talk about the formation of a kind of de facto alliance of various states in this space not in the future, but in the present.

Defence must rely on the implementation of the latest technology to

ensure information security.
In doing so, the agency relies on three principles. The first principle is the protection of "Internet freedom" and other network tools. The second is self-regulation in an open civil society and market economy. The third is to encourage "knowledge creation" and transparency.
The open network model and the mechanism of "communicating vessels" of the state and citizens require adaptation of the state to the new information realities of global scale, including at the institutional level. In the course of this adaptation, it is necessary not to forget that the state is not only an object, but also an active subject of the use of new technologies.
Thus, the goals of digital diplomacy should be seen as complementary to the political-military objectives of providing leadership in the global-information sphere.
Informatisation also poses new threats to leader states, increasing the asymmetric component of contemporary conflicts, leaving technologically advanced states vulnerable. The dual impact of ICTs on international security is manifested, on the one hand, in their contribution to democratisation and, consequently, to the reduction of conflict. On the other hand, information technologies are a convenient tool for creating asymmetric threats and increasing political influence, which results in provoking new armed clashes.

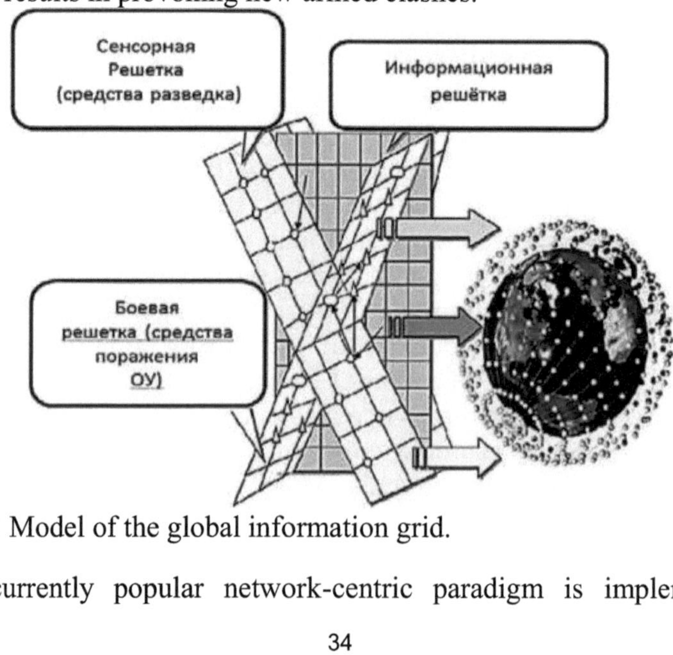

Fig.2.1 Model of the global information grid.

The currently popular network-centric paradigm is implemented through the basic functionality of matrix information-management systems, which includes the following main components: formation of a single coordinate-time field and linking to it all system elements, information agents, events, and data itself; collection and integration of heterogeneous information (in a single coordinate-time field) received from different sources with cross-refinement and addition; analysis and prediction of the situation development in the country; and analysis and forecasting of the situation in the country.

At the heart of this network-centric approach is the Global Information Grid (GIG), (Figure 2.1.) as a globally interconnected, end-to-end set of information that it accumulates, stores, distributes, and disseminates at the request of political and military actors. The GIG includes owned and leased communications, computer systems and services, software (and its applications), data, security services, other related services, and national security systems.

In their activities, the media and MCs use such principles of material selection, which are poorly compatible with in-depth analytical reporting and often hinder the creation of an information picture of the world that is more or less adequate to reality. In general, these principles are formulated as follows.

1. Priority (real and imaginary) and attractiveness of the topic for citizens. In accordance with this principle, the most frequent messages of mass media and media outlets deal with such problems as, for example, threat to peace and security of citizens, terrorism, environmental and other disasters, etc.

2. The uncommonness of the facts. This means that information about other extreme events - famines, wars, crimes, etc. - dominates over the coverage of everyday life phenomena. This explains, in particular, the tendency of the media and media organisations to negative information and sensationalism.

3. Novelty of facts. Reports that are not yet widely known can attract the attention of the population to a greater extent. This can be the latest data on the results of economic development or the number of unemployed, on the flight to other planets, on new political parties and their leaders, etc.

4. Success. According to this principle, programmes and articles include reports on the successes of political leaders, parties or entire states. Special attention is paid to the winners of elections or rating polls. The cult of stars in politics, art, sports is a typical phenomenon

for media and MCs in a market society.

5. High public status. The higher the status of the source of information, the more significant the interview or programme is considered to be, as it is assumed that its popularity, other things being equal, is directly proportional to the social status of the people reporting the information.

By virtue of this rule, the persons who have the easiest access to the media and MCs are those who occupy the highest positions in the political, military, church or other hierarchies: presidents, military chiefs, ministers, etc. They are devoted to the front pages of newspapers and the main radio and TV programmes. The front pages of newspapers and the main radio and television programmes are devoted to them.

Thus, public diplomacy is a generalised notion denoting the activities of various actors, both governmental and non-governmental, which are designed to explain to the foreign public the foreign policy pursued by a country and to induce a foreign state to make its foreign policy decisions in the direction that is favourable to these actors. In other words, public diplomacy is a system of dialogue with the foreign public.

§2.2 Classification of Threats to Information Resources in Inter-State Relations

Information security (IS) of an individual, society, state and modern automated and telecommunication systems is understood as the state of protection of the information environment corresponding to the interests (needs) of an individual, society and state in the information sphere, when their formation, use and development opportunities are ensured regardless of the presence of internal and external threats.

Information security is determined by the ability of the state (society, individual):

- to ensure with a certain probability sufficient and protected information resources and information flows to maintain its life activity and viability, sustainable functioning and development;
- to resist information dangers and threats, negative information impacts on individual and public consciousness and psyche of people, as well as on computer networks and other technical sources of information; to develop personal and group skills and abilities of safe behaviour;
- maintain constant readiness for adequate measures in the

information confrontation, no matter who imposes it.

The current situation required the improvement of the system of measures to counter foreign intelligence. Countering technical intelligence has become a task of national importance and an integral part of the overall system of measures to preserve state and official secrets.

In the current conditions, taking into account the considered threats to the IS of an individual, society and the state, it is important to consider the problems and tasks of ensuring IS, which is an integral part of ensuring the national security of any state of the world community at a new stage of its development - the stage of formation of the information society.

External threats, which are caused by the competitive nature of the development of interstate and international relations. Accordingly, there are also internal threats, largely related to the insufficient implementation of economic, socio-political and other reforms in the field of IS. The concept of national security refers to them as prerequisites for the emergence of threats. Taking into account these prerequisites, in our opinion, the sources of internal threats can include:

- backwardness of RUz in the sphere of informatisation of state authorities;
- imperfection of the system of organisation of state authorities on formation and implementation of a unified state policy of IS provision;
- criminalisation of social relations and the growth of organised crime;
- The increase in terrorism;
- aggravation of interethnic and foreign relations.

In order to neutralise information threats, there is a historically established system for the preservation of state secrets, including subsystems:

- of a cryptographic network of confidential communications;
- countering foreign technical intelligence;
- secrecy regime at closed state facilities.

Summarising the brief analysis of existing threats to confidential information, we can distinguish two directions of threats that reduce information security.

The first, traditionally developed within the framework of the protection of confidential information, represents the impacts that contribute to unauthorised access to this information. The second, developed within the framework of a broad understanding of IS issues, is related to the use of modern technical and organisational systems, as well as to the participation of people, teams of people and society as a whole and their exposure to external, negative information impacts.

Thus, it has been theoretically proved and repeatedly confirmed by practice that human psyche and thinking are subject to external informational influences and, if properly organised, it is possible to program human behaviour. Moreover, recently, methods and means of computer penetration into subconsciousness are being developed in order to have a deep impact on it. Therefore, the problem of not only information protection, but also protection from destructive impact of information, which acquires international scale and strategic character, is urgent. Due to the change in the concept of strategic arms development, which determines that the armed solution of world problems is becoming impossible, the concept of information warfare is more and more firmly entering into use.

There are threats that originate from unauthorised hardware and software. Such threats include, for example, the introduction of Trojans into the system: *keyloggers, sniffer and* others. A keylogger is a software product (module) or hardware device that registers keystrokes on a computer keyboard and then, as a rule, sends the keystroke log to an external resource to which an attacker has access. A sniffer is a hardware and software complex designed to intercept network traffic for the purpose of its subsequent analysis. As a rule, keyloggers and sniffers are installed to identify accounts and authentication mechanisms for access to certain IS resources.

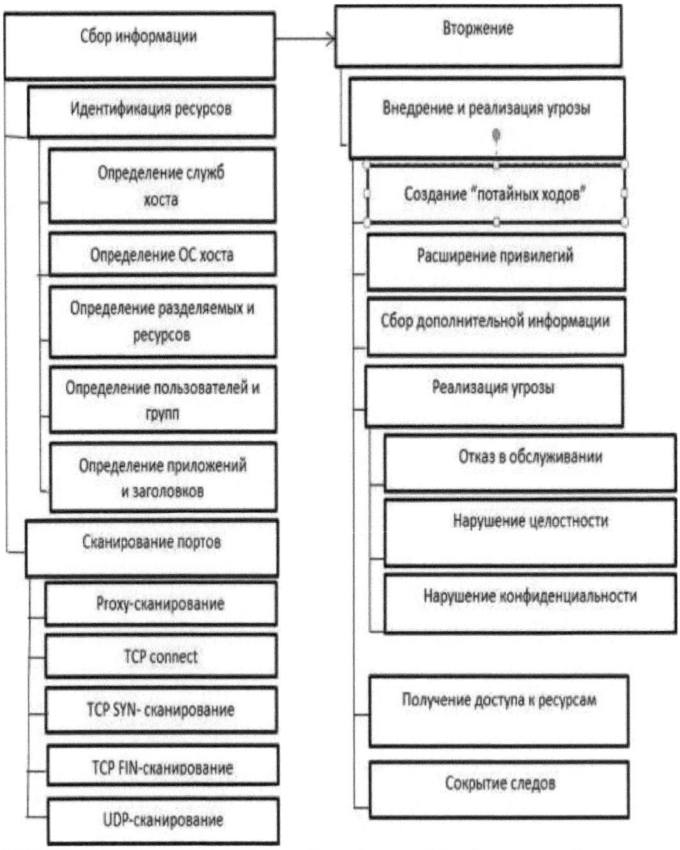

Fig.2.2 The process of threat realisation with the use of cross-network communication

Threat realisation (Fig.2.2) may be aimed at violation of confidentiality, relevance, integrity and availability of information (including violation of IS or its elements). The process of threat realisation generally consists of four stages:

- information gathering;
- intrusion (penetration of the operating environment);
- unauthorised access;
- elimination of traces of unauthorised access.

During the information gathering phase, an intruder may be interested in a variety of information about the IP, including:

- the topology of the network in which the system operates. In this case, the area around the network may be investigated (e.g., an intruder may be interested in the addresses of trusted but less secure

hosts);
- about the type of OS deployed in the IC;
- services running on the hosts, application software versions.

Identifying services executing on hosts can be done remotely by detecting "open ports";
- about IS subjects (users, administrators), their powers, moral and ethical principles, etc..;
- the IS-related policies applied in the organisation under study (e.g. access control policies, backup policies, etc.).

An analysis of the results of research on threats to information allows us to assert that one of the main threats to state security is attempts by Western intelligence services to extract confidential information constituting state, industrial, banking and other types of secrets. Leading Western countries continue to modernise and develop their intelligence services, improve technical intelligence, and increase its capabilities.

Ensuring the national security of the state (nation) consists in fulfilling two functions - the function of protecting a certain object containing the most important values of the state, which are the basis of vital interests of the individual, society and the state, and the function of developing this object. Or, using the terms of the National Security Strategy - realising strategic national priorities.

The totality of national interests is shown in the figure (Figure 2.3.).

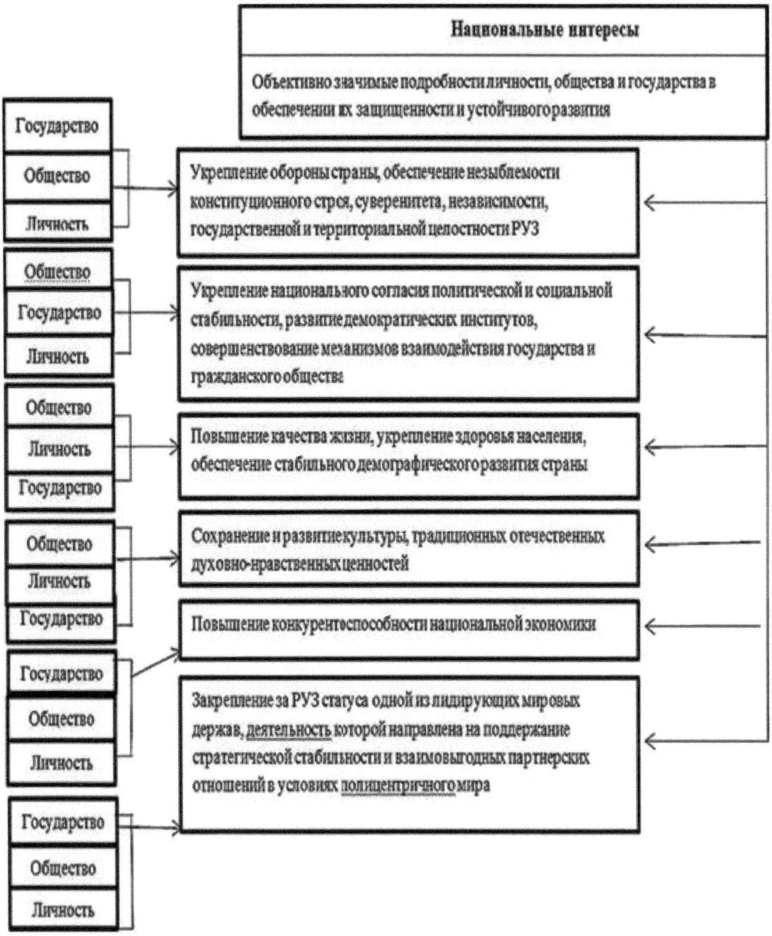

Fig.2.3. The totality of national interests.

Threats to the vital interests of an individual, society and the state can be conditionally divided into three groups (Figure 2.4.).

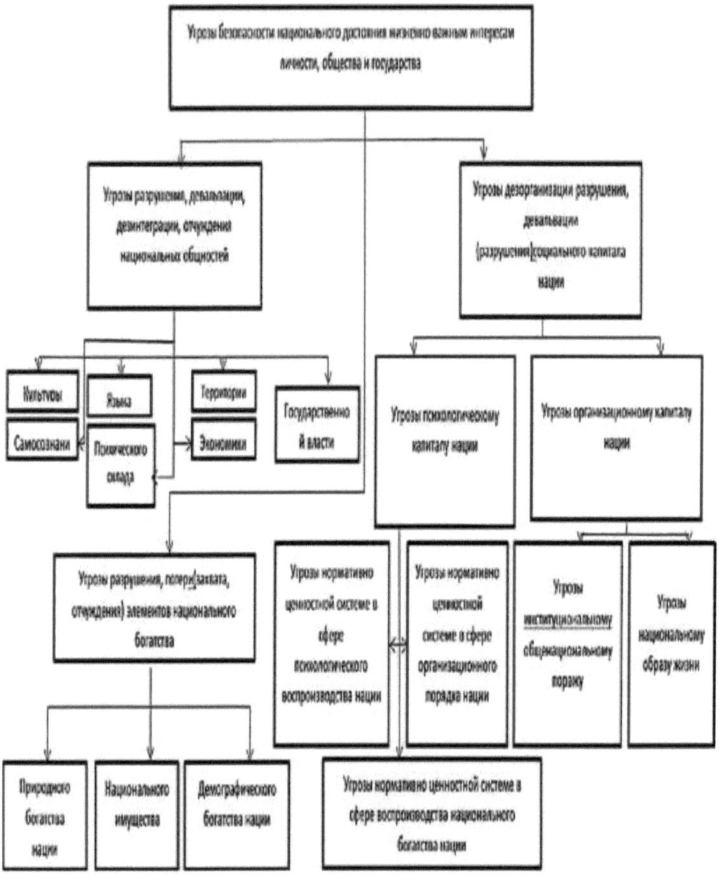

Figure 2.4. Threats to the vital interests of the individual, society and the state.

The following threats can be considered (Figure 2.5.):

1. In relation to the functions of ensuring national security - threats to the security of the existence of the state, society and the individual and threats to the possibility of sustainable development of the country, combined threats, combining threats to the security of the existence of the state, society and the individual and threats to the possibility of sustainable development of the country.
2. In relation to the object of security - external, internal and cross-border.
3. By scale of threats - global, regional, local.
4. By the nature and genesis of threats - natural (natural), anthropogenic.

The proposed general classifiers of threats to national security can be supplemented and detailed in accordance with the objectives of the study of national security problems and its elements.

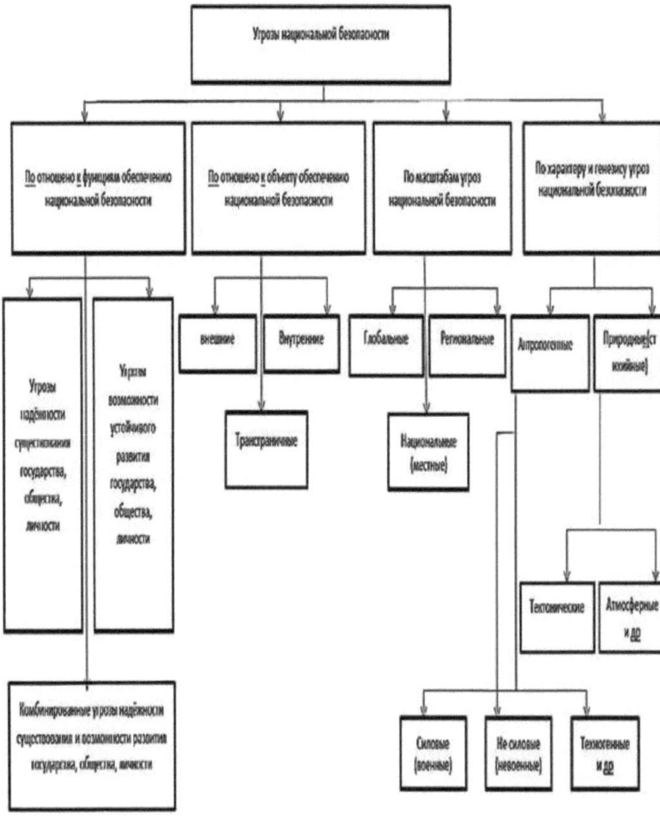

Fig.2.5. General classification of threats to national security

Throughout human history, the practice of ensuring the security of some States and peoples to the detriment of the interests and security of others has generated a continuous chain of wars and armed conflicts.

It has become increasingly clear that humanity requires a new dimension of security. In modern conditions, it is no longer sufficient to understand national security as merely the physical and moral-political ability of a State to protect itself from external sources of threat to its existence, since it has become definitively clear that ensuring national security is interlinked with ensuring international security and with maintaining and consolidating universal peace.

We are talking about possible deformations of the mass information system and the dissemination of disinformation leading to potential disturbances in social stability, harm to the health and lives of citizens as a result of propaganda or agitation inciting social, racial, national or religious hatred and hostility, and the activities of totalitarian sects promoting violence and cruelty.

Information weapons should be understood as any means and methods used for the purpose of damaging information resources, processes and systems of the State, negative information impact on defence, managerial, political, social, economic and other critical systems of the State, as well as massive psychological processing of the population with the aim of destabilising society and the State.

Currently, in a number of "Third World" countries, the prevailing view of information warfare is a set of propaganda actions affecting the cultural and attitudinal level, using the information opportunities provided by the processes of globalisation and public accessibility of the media. These two points of view are certainly polar and do not reflect the entire spectrum of views on information warfare, but they give a clear picture of the significant differences in the perception of the structure of risks arising from the development of information technologies.

Cyberspace has no borders, and therefore no statehood. And here state security issues can only be addressed as international security issues.

The author's aim is to identify the reasons for the close attention to the problem of information security, to determine its place in the structure of security as a whole and to analyse to what extent the existing system of international law is capable of countering emerging and potential threats to international information security.

The development of the information image of warfare, for which "perception management" is so important, leads to paradoxical effects. On the one hand, propaganda methods are constantly improving. On the other hand, it is becoming increasingly difficult to get the desired effect from their use, because the media and means of communication have become so advanced that it is increasingly difficult to use them to disseminate the right information and only in the right direction. Diverse flows of information precede the conflict and can play an important role in its development.

Globalisation has had the same effect: it has weakened nation states and encouraged the emergence of broader groupings in which the notion of human rights has become dominant. An important consequence of globalisation has been the gradual disappearance of former sources of conflict, in particular conflicts over claims to territory and natural wealth.

In information warfare, one has to think more and more not about questions of strategy or territory conquest, but about the information components of warfare, because today this aspect of organised violence is becoming critical.

In warfare, the information component is gaining much more weight, its role is becoming clearer, and its scope of use is broader than in the era of industrialised warfare. Information permeates the entire structure of the war machine, whether it is the use of satellites to monitor opponents, computers that store data and assess any army's needs, or "smart" weapons that are programmed so that the only thing left to do is "shoot and forget". Thus, information is no longer just a matter of intelligence gathering information about the enemy and its resources, it is now embedded in the weapons themselves and in the systems that make decisions.

Certain types of information-psychological influence, addressed to the population as a whole or addressed to specific individuals, social strata and groups, political parties and movements, are capable of seriously disrupting the normal and vital activities of social institutions, state structures, public organisations, associations of citizens and individuals.

In this purpose, quite different weapons can act as information weapons: high-precision weapons for the defeat of control organs or separate radio-electronic means, means of electronic warfare (REB), sources of powerful electromagnetic pulse, software viruses, etc.

Information weapons can be divided into three categories by type of impact: information technology-based weapons, energy-based weapons and chemical weapons.

Examples of energy-based information weapons are:

- High-precision homing munitions, including specialised cruise missiles and strike drones;
- means of forceful radio-electronic suppression, high-powered microwave generators, means of forceful influence through power grids;
- ground and airborne electronic warfare equipment, jamming transmitters;
- special radiation generators that affect the human psyche.

The use of information technology as an information weapon is considered the most promising. Information technologies are an integral part of high-precision munitions, as their guidance is provided by systems of location and reconnaissance by visual, radar, and other demasking features. Therefore, it is reasonable to consider these functional subsystems as information weapons as well.

Sources of threats to international information security include:

- the presence of countries striving for dominance in the global information sphere, intensifying international competition for the possession of technological and information resources and their markets;
- active activities of international terrorist and other criminal communities, organisations and groups;
- the persistence of the technological gap between the world's leading powers, exacerbating the dependence of countries with a lower level of development on the purchase of foreign equipment to ensure the functioning of their critical infrastructures and increasing the ability of monopolists to impede the creation of nationally competitive modern information technologies;
- "arms race" in the information sphere, the development of military science towards the development and adoption by States of concepts of "information wars", the creation of means of destructive impact on the information spheres of other countries of the world, disruption of the normal functioning of information and telecommunications systems, the preservation of information resources or gaining unauthorised access to them, as well as the imposition of information.

Clarification of the nature of the behaviour associated with the use of information means of influence and qualified as a violation of the principle of non-use of force and, at the same time, as a ground for self-defence and coercive measures, is related to the formulation in the Definition of Aggression of the criteria whose presence in specific cases of the use of force.

Thus, any use of information means for destructive purposes in an interstate conflict can be qualified as an act of aggression, regardless of the route and territory from which it was committed. Moreover, the use of the territory of a third State for these purposes entails only its involvement in the conflict, but not the transfer of responsibility for aggression to it.

§2.3 Classification of Confidential Information Resources of Objects in Interstate Information Security

The most important result of the formation of the information society at the turn of the century was the emergence of the global information space, in which a fierce struggle for achieving information superiority has developed. The security of information and the information environment is a factor that actively influences the national security of states. At the same time, attacks on critical infrastructure of states are becoming more and more sophisticated. The number of cases of ICTs being used to spread the ideas of extremism and terrorism and to commit cross-border crimes involving the violation of human rights and freedoms is growing worldwide.

The information space and cyberspace are gradually becoming practically a "war zone". The problem of information security has become a global issue due to the real possibility of using the potential of the latest ITC to ensure military and political superiority, forceful confrontation and blackmail.

Information security is today a critical component of national, regional and international security.

In today's world, everything is dialectical, as a result of which negative social, cultural and economic factors (cybercrime, cyberterrorism, information wars, etc.) are becoming a side effect of technological progress, with information and digital inequality, legal uncertainty and impunity acting as a breeding ground. In order to continue the progressive development of the information society, it is necessary to ensure effective counteraction to the threats of the use of modern information technologies to disrupt peace and security, commit crimes, prepare and carry out terrorist acts and disseminate terrorist ideology in the practice of resolving the contradictions of social development. Due to the transboundary nature of threats to information security, such work should be carried out both at the national level and from the standpoint of international (regional) co-operation.

The Open Systems Interconnection Basic Reference Model (OSI) is used for IS interaction. The OSI model divides the means of interaction into seven layers (Table 1). Each layer deals with a very specific aspect of the interaction of network devices. The OSIoπucbiβaeτ model only deals with system communications, not with end-user applications. Applications implement their own communication protocols by referring to system facilities. In doing so, an application may take over the functions of some of the upper layers of the OSI model. In this case, when interconnection is required, it directly accesses the system tools that perform the functions of the lower layers of the OSI model.

Table 2.1. OSI model levels

Data type	Layer	Functions
Data	7. Application	Operation of application services
	6. Representative (presentation)	Data representation and encryption
	5. Session (session)	Session management
Segments	4. transport transport)	Direct connection between end points and reliability
Packages	3. Network	Route definition and logical addressing
Personnel	2. Channel (data link)	Physical addressing
Bits	1. Physical	Working with transmission medium, signals and binary data

According to the OS1 model standards, protocols must communicate either with protocols at their own level or with protocols one unit above and/or below their level. Interactions with protocols at their own level are called horizontal, and interactions with protocols one level above or one level below are called vertical. Protocols in the OSI model cannot perform the functions of protocols at another layer. Note that this rule is not enforced in alternative versions of internetworking models.

Clarification of the content of the concept of "information security" is facilitated by its decomposition by components: subject and purpose, which allows us to consider each of the elements. The element "information" characterises the phenomenon under study as relating to the information sphere. The element "security" provides a qualitative characteristic of the state of social relations, determining that there is no (or does not influence) undeclared external destructive impact on their development. Different ways of achieving this state are possible:

- "threat-resistant" relations - i.e. their property of not being subjected to changes when they are exposed to threats (immunity);
- "threat-protection" (achieved through the creation of a separate subsystem preventing, detecting and suppressing the destructive impact of threats on "basic" social relations);
- "invulnerability" - development in conditions of a priori incompatibility with the environment of threat realisation.

The first approach is based on the objective understanding of information security as a manifestation of the essential nature of information to preserve the stability of its properties under various negative influences (self-regulation function). In this context, information security is understood as ensuring sustainable development of basic institutions. This approach can be called "immune", which assumes modelling the subject's adaptability to environmental changes as the main method of implementation. In this sense, ensuring information security is "a permanent complex of legal, organisational, technological and technical services and conditions that create a safe functioning of all means of information security".

The main goal of the project is to develop an information infrastructure and interaction between information systems of public authorities, local self-governance, civil society structures, economy, and the realisation of citizens' rights in the information space of the state and in global information systems, including the Internet".

The second approach is based on the recognition of the subjective nature of information security. In this case, information security is aimed at creating a barrier between the interests and threats to the interests of specific subjects of relations. The subjective understanding of information security forms the basis of activity, value (axiological) and other definitions of information security as a derivative of national interests. The above approach can be called "defensive". The main method of ensuring information security in this case is the regime method, providing the construction of a system of regulations of behaviour of subjects of relations.

The third approach is based on the definition of information security as an activity to eliminate emerging threats at different stages of their origin and development. Here, information security is aimed at identifying and neutralising threats and their sources and can be regarded as an "offensive" activity. Analytical and prognostic and preventive methods of ensuring information security are considered as the core methods. Within the framework of this approach, information security is ensured by a dedicated target subsystem.

The fourth approach can be considered the definition of information security as the creation of conditions in which threats do not affect the protected interests at all. Such a doubtful condition in terms of feasibility for social relations, nevertheless, allows us to consider this definition in the aspect of information security along with others, due to the technical and technological conditionality of this sphere of social relations.

Indeed, the possibility of transferring relationships to an artificial, technologically-driven environment is now beyond doubt. Consequently, this environment can be designed to be ahead of threats.

The science has formed a dominant concept of system-structural construction of information security ensuring, which allows to define its categorical content: rights and interests of subjects of relations - threats to the realisation of allocated interests - measures to counteract threats - security of interests. Legal support of information security, implemented in the system of legal acts (including model legislation), is designed to transfer the system of relations from the theoretical to the practical plane.

The following can be highlighted as the main limitations in the field of information security:

1) prohibitions on the dissemination of information of an extremist nature, pornographic content; information promoting the cult of violence and cruelty, containing calls for the violent overthrow of the constitutional order, containing calls for the organisation or holding of mass riots, calls for the unlawful organisation or holding of mass events; prohibitions on the dissemination of information containing information that could be used to cause harm to health or violate public safety, including information that could be used for the organisation or holding of mass events; prohibitions on the dissemination of information containing information that could be used to cause harm to health or violate public safety, including information that could be used for the organisation or holding of mass events

2) prohibitions on the collection of information containing the secrecy of a person's private life, personal data of a citizen, official information of limited dissemination (official secret), commercial secret, professional secret; prohibitions on the collection of information constituting state secrets, other information for transferring it to a foreign state, foreign organisation or their representative to the detriment of the national security of the state;

3) prohibitions on the use, in violation of the rights of its owners, of information constituting objects of copyright and related rights, industrial property rights, as well as on the use of malicious computer programmes;

4) prohibitions on restraining the free flow of information, including restricting the dissemination of publicly available information and exercising censorship.

Information resources hosted in open telecommunication systems have inherent characteristics that, to a large extent, negate their accessibility and anonymity, complicate the possibilities of control, etc. All of this allows terrorists, terrorist groups or other similar organisations to modify classic forms of terrorist activity and creates the possibility of using them to carry out terrorist offences and other illegal manifestations. All of this allows terrorists, terrorist groups or other similar organisations to modify classic forms of terrorist activity, and creates the possibility of using them to carry out terrorist crimes and other illegal manifestations capable of threatening the integrity of states and destabilising the international situation.

The phenomenon of state secrets (state secrets) is an objective reality in the sphere of interstate relations. Attacks on state secrets in developed states are considered as offences against the foundations of the constitutional order and security of the state.

By its nature, secrecy is not a simple and contradictory socio-legal phenomenon. In the legal interpretation, a secret is information to which access is restricted. A state secret is that part of information that is excluded from free circulation. It limits the constitutional rights of citizens, interests in scientific, economic and other spheres and leads to a conflict of interest, in which the priority is given to the interests of state security.

Under the current conditions, the prospect of reforming the institution of state secrets, revising its place in the system of ensuring national security, and revising the methods of its provision is foreseeable. There are several ways out of the current situation:

- borrowing the conceptual-legal platform for the protection of state secrets (secrecy) from other countries (blocs);
- elaboration of a universal international platform for the protection of state secrets (secrecy);
- development of national mechanisms for the protection of state secrets (secrecy) of states based on the exchange of methods and experience and, as a consequence, the development of international legal mechanisms for the protection of state secrets (secrecy).

The concept of "state secret" is defined as "information protected by the state in the field of military, foreign policy, economic, intelligence, counterintelligence and operational and investigative activities, the dissemination of which may harm security".

Official secret - information of the nature of separate data that may be part of a state secret, the disclosure or loss of which may cause damage to the national interests of the state, the interests of state bodies and organisations. Information constituting a state secret is assigned the secrecy grades "of special importance" and "top secret". Information constituting an official secret is assigned the classification "secret".

In the social sphere, there is a growing danger of the development of aggressive consumer ideology in society, total commercialisation of culture, spread of ideas of violence and intolerance, and destructive impact on people's psyche. Because of this, progressive and sustainable development of states is possible only if the proper level of information security and counteraction to sources of threats in the information sphere are fully ensured.

In the light of current global trends of social development, the use of information and communication technologies is becoming the main threats in the field of international information security:

а) as an information weapon for politico-military purposes contrary to international law;

б) to carry out hostile actions and acts of aggression aimed at discrediting sovereignty, violating the territorial integrity of States and posing a threat to international peace, security and strategic stability;

в) for terrorist purposes, including for destructive impact on elements of critical information infrastructure, as well as for the propaganda of terrorist ideas and the involvement of new actors in terrorist activities;

г) to interfere in the internal affairs of sovereign States, disturb public order, incite inter-ethnic, inter-racial and inter-confessional hatred, propagate racist and xenophobic ideas or theories that generate hatred and discrimination and incite violence;

д) to commit offences, including those related to unlawful access to computer information and the creation, use and distribution of malicious computer programmes.

International information security is defined in the Fundamentals as the state of the global information space that excludes the possibility of violating the rights of individuals, society and the State in the information sphere, as well as the possibility of destructive and unlawful influence on elements of the critical information infrastructure of a particular State.

The system of international information security is designed to counter threats to strategic stability and promote equal strategic partnership in the global information space requiring the following tasks:

а) formation of a system of international information security at various levels (bilateral, multilateral, regional and global);

б) Creating conditions that reduce the risk of using ICTs to carry out hostile actions, acts of aggression, discredit sovereignty, and violate the territorial integrity of states, thereby posing a threat to international peace, security and strategic stability;

в) Formation of international co-operation mechanisms to counter threats of ICT use for terrorist purposes;

г) Creating conditions to counter threats of ICTs for extremist purposes as well as interference in the internal affairs of sovereign states;

д) Increasing the effectiveness of international cooperation in countering computer crime;

е) Creating conditions for ensuring technological sovereignty of states in the field of ICT and overcoming information inequality between developing and developed countries.

§2.4 Methods of ensuring information security in interstate relations

General methods of ensuring information security are divided into legal, organisational-technical and economic.

Legal methods of ensuring information security include the development of normative legal acts regulating relations in the information sphere and normative methodological documents on information security issues.

Organisational and technical methods of ensuring information security are:

- creation and improvement of the information security system;
- development, use and improvement of information protection means and methods for controlling the effectiveness of these means, development of secure telecommunication systems, and improvement of the reliability of special software;
- creation of systems and means to prevent unauthorised access to processed information and special effects causing destruction, destruction, distortion of information;

- identification of technical devices and programmes that pose a danger to the normal functioning of information and telecommunications systems;
- certification of information protection means, licensing of activities in the field of protection of state secrets, standardisation of methods and means of information protection;
- control over personnel actions in protected information systems, training in the field of information security;
- formation of a system for monitoring indicators and characteristics of the country's information security in the most important spheres of life and activities of society and the state.

Economic methods of information security include:

- developing information security programmes and determining the procedure for their financing;
- improvement of the system for financing work related to the implementation of legal and organisational-technical methods of information protection, and the creation of a system for insuring the information of individuals and legal entities. The state policy of ensuring information security determines the main directions of activity of state authorities and government bodies in this area, the procedure for fixing their duties to protect the country's interests in the information sphere within the framework of their areas of activity and is based on the observance of the balance of interests of the individual, society and the state in the information sphere.

General principles of organisation of protection of confidential information applied in the development of protection systems:

- Continuity;
- Sufficiency;
- Comprehensiveness;
- Consistency;
- Efficiency;

Measures to counter security threats include legal, moral and ethical, technological, physical and technical.

All these tasks help in achieving the goals of timely threat detection, operational prevention, neutralisation or suppression, threat containment, attack repelling and threat destruction.

When protecting acoustic information, it is necessary to choose the most favourable conditions for the location of the protected premises, to establish the length of the controlled area, to limit the admission of employees to the protected premises, to conduct special inspections of both the protected premises and the technical means located in it. In addition, it is possible to apply information protection systems, sound and vibration isolation, shielding, use of certified technical means, localisation of connecting lines within the controlled area, disconnection of technical means from the line and power supply.

Active and passive means of protection of speech information are also used.

The active ones include:

- Vibro acoustic noise generators;
- Electromagnetic noise generators (low frequency, high frequency);

The passive ones include:

- Sound and vibration insulation;
- Shielding structures;
- filters;
- Galvanic isolation and disconnection devices.

When protecting speech information from leakage due to VTSS, signal filtering, noise cancellation and disconnection of the signal propagation circuit are used.

Technical means of protection include hardware, software, cryptographic means of protection, which hinder the possibility of an attack, help to detect the fact of its occurrence, get rid of the consequences of the attack.

Technical means of security subsystems of modern distributed information systems fulfil the following main functions:

- Authentication of communication partners to ensure that the partner is authentic when establishing a connection;
- Information source authentication to verify the authenticity of the message source;
- access control to protect against unauthorised use of resources;
- data confidentiality, which provides protection against unauthorised acquisition of information;
- Data integrity, which enables the detection and, in some cases, the prevention of alteration of information during its storage and transmission;
- affiliation, which provides proof that the information belongs to a particular person.

The following mechanisms are used to realise the above functions:

- encryption, which converts information into a form that cannot be understood by unauthorised users;

- An electronic digital signature that transfers the properties of a real signature to electronic documents;
- Access control mechanisms that manage the process of accessing user resources based on information such as access control databases, passwords, security labels, access times, access routes, and access durations;
- integrity control mechanisms that control the integrity of both a single message and a stream of messages, using checksums, special labels, message sequence numbers, and cryptographic methods;
- Authentication mechanisms that decide whether a user is who he or she claims to be based on passwords, authenticating devices or biometrics presented by the user;
- traffic augmentation mechanisms that add additional information to the message stream, "masking" useful information from the attacker;
- Notarisation mechanisms that serve to authenticate the source of information.

The modern stage of development of this problem is characterised by a transition from its traditional representation as a problem of information protection to a broader understanding - the problem of information security, which consists in its complex solution in two main directions.

The first is the protection of state secrets and confidential information, which mainly ensures the impossibility of unauthorised access to them. At the same time, confidential information means information of limited access of public nature (commercial secrets, party secrets, etc.).

The second area includes defence against information, which has recently become international in scope and strategic in nature. There are three main areas of defence against so-called information weapons (influence):

- on technical systems and facilities;
- Society;
- the human psyche.

In accordance with this approach, sets of information threats, functions and classes of information protection tasks are specified and supplemented.

All methods of defence according to the guidance documentation are

divided into two groups, such as concealment and disinformation.
The hiding group includes:
- Passive concealment - consists in excluding or significantly hindering the detection of objects;
- active concealment - in creating to technical means of reconnaissance masking noise interference of various physical nature and false situation by physical fields;
- special protection - consists in scrambling of telephone conversations, encoding of digital information by cryptographic methods, software methods of information modification.

The misinformation group includes:
- technical misinformation;
- imitation;
- Legendising.

The principles of information security engineering include:
- secrecy of information protection;
- reliability of information protection;
- continuity of defence;
- rationality of defence;
- integrated application of various methods and means of defence;
- diversity of defences;
- cost-effective defence.

Types of information protection against leakage through technical channels.

A number of means are used to protect information from leakage and reduce parasitic links through technical channels:

Shielding of electromagnetic waves.

Shielding is the localisation of electromagnetic energy within a certain space by blocking its propagation.

An isolation filter is a device that limits the propagation of interference on wires common to the source and receiver of the interference.

The use of quality screens allows to solve many problems, including protection of information in premises and technical channels, electromagnetic compatibility of equipment and devices when used together, protection of personnel from increased levels of electromagnetic fields and ensuring safe environmental conditions around working electrical installations and microwave devices.

Security of fibre optic cabling systems.

Fibre optics - is ordinary glass that transmits electromagnetic energy in the infrared wavelength range. There is virtually no radiation to the outside. Effective information capture is only possible by direct physical connection to the fibre optic line. But if WOSPI is considered as a system as a whole, containing workstations, interface cards, servers, hubs and other network active devices, which are themselves a direct source of radiation, the problem of information leakage becomes relevant. Therefore, when deciding on the use of fibre optic cabling systems (FOCS), this factor cannot be ignored.

Along with the listed common features, fibre optic cables of different models can have additional binding tapes, anti-corrosive and waterproof windings, corrugated metal sheaths, etc.

Cryptographic methods of information protection.

The method of transformation in a cryptographic system corresponds to the use of a special algorithm. The action of such an algorithm is triggered by a unique number (a sequence of bits), usually called a cipher key.

For most systems, the key generator circuitry may be a set of instructions and commands, or a piece of hardware, or a computer program, or all of these together, but in any case the encryption (decryption) process is implemented only by this special key. In order for the exchange of encrypted data to be successful, both the sender and the receiver need to know the correct key setting and keep it secret.

Asymmetric cryptosystems, also called public-key systems, are considered to be the most promising cryptographic data protection systems today. Their essence is that the key used for encryption is different from the decryption key. The encryption key is not secret and can be known to all users of the system. However, decryption using a known decryption key is not possible. A special, secret key is used for decryption. Knowledge of the public key does not allow the secret key to be determined. Thus, only the recipient of the message, who possesses this secret key, can decrypt the message.

Several public key cryptosystems are known. The most developed today is the RSA system. RSA is a system of collective use, in which each user has his own keys for encryption and decryption of data, and only the decryption key is secret.

Methods of information protection using holography are an actual and developing direction. Holography is a section of science and technology engaged in the study and creation of methods, devices for recording and processing of waves of different nature. Optical holography is based on the phenomenon of wave interference. Wave interference is observed in the distribution of waves in space and slow spatial distribution of the resulting wave. The pattern arising at wave interference contains information about the object. If this pattern is fixed on a photosensitive surface, a hologram is formed. When the hologram or its section is irradiated with a reference wave, a three-dimensional three-dimensional image of the object can be seen. Holography is applicable to waves of any nature and nowadays finds more and more practical application for identification of products of various purposes.

Means of ensuring information security on the Internet.

Security is based on cryptosystems with a pair of keys (public and private). The public key is available to many people in the process of encrypting the information that will be sent to the holder of this key pair. Also, with the help of the public key, users can decrypt the information that they receive from the owner of the key. The private key should only be available to its owner, who can use it to decrypt messages encrypted with the public key. The private key can also be used for encryption.

The digital signature method ensures that the sender is authentic and the message is not tampered with. A cached and private-key encrypted message (digest) is transmitted together with the original message. The recipient decrypts the digest with the public key and generates the cache. If the digests are identical, the message was actually sent by the key owner and was not modified during transmission. Thus, the encrypted digest of the message serves as a digital signature. The following two digest derivation algorithms (MDA) are most commonly used: MD5, developed by RSA Laboratories, generates a 128-bit digest; SHA-1 (Secure Hash Algorithm), developed by NIST (National Institute of Standards and Technonlogy) and NSA (National Security Agency), generates a 160-bit digest.

A public key system provides authentication by key, but does not guarantee that the key belongs to a specific owner. Certificate - a digital document certifying that a given key belongs to a given person (organisation, server).

§2.5 Methods for securing critical information infrastructures

Various information systems are already storing and processing significant amounts of information, including those related to issues of state policy and defence, financial and scientific and technical spheres, and the private lives of citizens.

At the same time, criminal, terrorist and intelligence attacks by individuals, communities, foreign intelligence services and organisations can be equally dangerous.

In international practice, the categories of critical information infrastructure (CII) found in the classifications of the vast majority of states generally include:

- nuclear facilities;
- power grids, power generating and power distribution facilities;
- transport systems: aviation, railways, roads, etc.;
- facilities for production and storage of agricultural products, as well as food supply;
- public administration and government communications facilities;
- facilities of the fuel and energy complex (FEC - heat and energy complexes), including oil and gas complexes;
- basic telecommunication systems, networks, hardware and software and communication systems;
- OPK facilities (OPK - Experimental Isolation Complexes) (chemically hazardous facilities);
- financial and credit sector;
- water supply and water supply;
- Health care.

The information and telecommunication environments can be distinguished as part of the CII.

KII information environment is a set of computing and information resources that form the ACS of critical facilities. In this case, computing resources are formed by a set of local area networks, other computer facilities and software describing methods and techniques of information processing automation, and can be used to organise distributed computing (e.g., for deciphering encrypted code, modelling complex social and physical processes).

The telecommunication environment of KII is formed by a set of telecommunication devices; communication lines and channel-forming equipment; systems of open protocols for information exchange between telecommunication devices; a global system of digital addresses and domain names (digital identifiers); software that implements methods, algorithms and processes of telecommunication communication on the basis of protocols of interaction of local computer networks and provides access to local computer networks and other means of autonomous communication.

Taking into account the main tasks of the international information security system development, the following main groups of international relations can be distinguished:

Defining the boundaries of national CII in the global information and communication infrastructure;

consolidation of signs of computer incidents in the automated control systems of the KVO;

international co-operation in the field of computer incident response in the KVO.

In recent years, Western experts, recognising the possibility of a direct threat of nuclear strikes on the territory of the United States, Western Europe and Japan, have paid special attention to assessing the impact on the vital facilities of their countries by non-nuclear means and the possible consequences of these impacts on the political, economic, environmental and other spheres of state activity. It is obvious that in the conditions of today's extremely intensive development of the infrastructure of leading foreign countries, there are many so-called critical facilities, such as large hydraulic structures, oil, gas, and product pipelines, nuclear power plant networks, storage points for strategic oil and gas reserves, harmful chemical industries, transport hubs, airfields, etc., the disabling of which can lead to unpredictable severe and even catastrophic consequences.

In the proposed review, the list of identified critical facilities does not include traditional types of military facilities - missile bases and ranges, air bases, higher state and military administration bodies, since according to researchers' assessments these facilities have a sufficiently high degree of protection and are practically not vulnerable to the impact of conventional means of destruction.

The main threat to the country's vital activity is the disabling of facilities, resulting in disruption of transport and energy systems, water supply, etc. on the scale of the country or individual districts.

The protection of critical facilities (CFIs) and their aggregate, commonly referred to as critical infrastructure, or critical infrastructure for short, is one of the most important tasks for ensuring the national security of any country. The protection of critical infrastructure includes measures to ensure its preservation in the event of various natural or man-made impacts. The greatest danger at present is terrorism. The experience of recent events in the world shows that the danger of terrorism is constantly increasing.

The following factors contribute to the difficulties in combating terrorism:

- conventional warfare is the exact opposite of terrorist asymmetric warfare;
- as a rule, the organisational structure of terrorist organisations does not allow them to be quickly detected and promptly dismantled;
- identification of offenders is often difficult;
- The doctrine of terrorism is interethnic and in opposition to state power;
- the chain of links within terrorist organisations is convoluted and amorphous;
- The scale of terrorist logistics is relatively small, making them difficult to trace;
- requirements for detecting individual fighters and reconnaissance of terrorist bases may vary considerably in different environments.

The Security Management System (SMS) provides:

- receipt by higher authorities of all necessary information from any subordinate or co-operating control body (point) located anywhere in the country;
- automated preparation of data for operational planning and decision-making on the use of available forces and means, including in combined teams;
- technical interoperability of communication systems and automated data processing of all agencies, and collection of information in near-real time;
- automated processing and delivery to consumers of all generated information (including intelligence) necessary for operational planning and decision-making;
- interoperability at all levels of management links; information closure and protection; circular broadcasting and processing of consumer requests for information.

Priorities for the U.S. CWO security system are:

- preservation of life and minimisation of health risks to citizens;
- preventing terrorist threats;
- detection of presence, assessment of readiness to use, control of the movement of weapons of mass destruction;
- detection, decontamination and decontamination, transport and destruction of hazardous substances, prevention of secondary effects

of such substances;
- The public dissemination of information from any representative bodies and agencies responsible for the response about emerging threats, emergencies through adequate and reliable systems and means of communication;
- Maintaining and preparing the necessary security and recovery assets;
- carrying out activities to rehabilitate the facilities.

Ensuring the reliable and responsive management of the security system is a major task that is defined in advance of day-to-day operations and described in advance directives and emergency response plans. Management is tailored to the historical management structure of a particular level, agency or state, depending on the complexity of the situation, available capabilities and resources. State, state, and local management systems are coordinated and take into account the flexibility of the response to the situation to optimise the allocation of forces and resources across facilities and time. Considerable attention is given to integrating the various levels of systems and taking full advantage of the benefits that each provides.

The same principles apply to the security systems of PMCs in different countries, while the way they operate also has many common features and characteristics. The differences are determined by the priorities chosen at and the peculiarities of the state's internal structure, with the country's leadership assessing the list of threats and their scale playing an important role.

Closed communication channels are used to collect information to ensure the secure transmission of classified information. Closure may be accomplished through commercial methods. Information from the private sector and the information distribution centre may not be closed.

Review and analysis is a critical part of the detection and alerting process and should be carried out in a manner that ensures the timeliness, accuracy and reliability of the information received. Personnel may interact through telephone and electronic contacts to obtain complete, clear and verified information with various authorities. The success of a disaster prevention centre depends on the ability of analysts to analyse and anticipate threats. In order to improve the defence system, it is envisaged to implement a decision support system - Homeland Security Advisory System, which is a unified threat warning system that effectively distributes risk information to all levels of government, as well as ensuring that it is communicated to the public. The system will assess how realistic a threat is, whether it is corroborated by various sources, its characteristics, severity and scale. Five threat levels are established:

1. Low ("green").
2. Possible ("blue").
3. Rising ("yellow").
4. High ("orange").
5. Obviously high ("red").

Each degree corresponds to a corresponding set of measures. This system allows you to assess how likely a threat is to occur using a five-point system.

Risk assessment involves combining information related to threats, vulnerability of facilities and possible consequences. Risk management is based on the organisation of protection measures through the development of a risk mitigation strategy. Many models and methodologies have been developed with consideration of the use of available resources on the basis of the efficiency-value criterion. Most methodologies include the following elements to a greater or lesser extent:

- Identification of important sites and identification of those that may be considered to be KVOs;
- Identifying, describing and assessing threats;
- assessing the vulnerability of the IED to various specific classes of threats;
- Risk identification (i.e., the expected consequences of specific types of attacks on specific types of targets);
- identifying ways to reduce emerging risks;
- prioritising risk reduction measures on the basis of the developed strategy.

CONCLUSIONS TO CHAPTER II

In this chapter:

- The main priority principles of digital diplomacy and the model of the global information grid are presented;
- Threat factors of information resources in interstate relations are classified;
- threats to national security are considered:

(a) In relation to national security functions;
б) in relation to the security object;
в) on the scale of the threats;
г) by the nature and genesis of the threats;

- classified confidential information resources of objects in interstate information security;
- The main limitations in the sphere of ensuring national information security are highlighted;
- methods of ensuring information security in interstate relations are given;
- methods of ensuring the security of critical information infrastructures are defined.

CHAPTER III

CONCEPTUAL MODELS FOR ENSURING INFORMATION SECURITY INTERSTATE RELATIONS

The third chapter "Conceptual models of ensuring information security of interstate relations" is an exclusive material, where the author's approaches to the study of organisational and legal problems of formation of the system of ensuring information security of interstate relations, as well as international information security, where the social aspects related to the philosophical content of the concept of "secrecy" are considered in a concentrated form, where the correlation between all types of secrets is shown. This chapter also proposes algorithms for regulating the strategy of interstate relations on the basis of digital diplomacy.

§3.1 Formation of interstate regimes of the integrated information security system

Integrated security systems are a set of technical means of protection and security of the object, united on the basis of a single software package in a common information environment with a single database. An integrated intelligent security and facility management system typically includes:

- Digital video surveillance system;
- Access control and management system;
- Fire alarm system;
- Safety and process control subsystems;
- Life Support Systems.

An integrated security system (ISS) is a complex of equipment that operates according to common protocols, uses common communication lines and databases, and is controlled from a single software core. Such integration allows setting up automatic reactions of one ISMS subsystem to events recorded by another subsystem.

The structure of the integrated security system is a central microprocessor unit with an operator terminal and a printer connected via communication lines to the controllers of certain subsystems (peripheral part).

The security of any facility has its own specifics. Designing an integrated security system is strictly individualised to a specific object. The properties of the object almost completely determine the final type of the optimal ISIS for it. Ways to form a technical system of enterprise security largely depend on the characteristics of enclosing structures, premises and engineering systems of the object, their compliance with the requirements of regulatory and technical documentation, conceptual provisions of security. It is also necessary to take into account the current operational situation in the area where the enterprise is located. Only by taking into account the whole complex of external factors, it is possible to achieve a sufficiently high level of safety.

Based on the goal of building an effective protection of the enterprise, the most appropriate solution is to use the principles of system integration and the creation of a complex multifunctional technical system, combining on the basis of modern information technology and hardware and software integration of several subsystems, functionally and informationally related to each other, and their work according to a single algorithm.

An important part of the ISB is the connecting lines, through which information from the peripheral subsystems is transmitted to the central monitoring desk.

The following can be used as ISB communication lines: radio lines;
of the power wires of the power supply network;
of wired twisted pairs;
of telephone wires;
coaxial cables;
fibre optic cables.

Classification of protected information by degree of secrecy (confidentiality):

of special importance (especially important) - OV;
top secret (strictly confidential) - SS;
secret (confidential) - S;
for official use (not for printing, sent to the list) - CPD;
unclassified (open).

Information security threats can be classified according to their orientation as follows:

a) for the individual:

- violation of the constitutional rights and freedoms of citizens to seek, receive, transmit, produce and disseminate objective information;
- deprivation of the right of citizens to privacy;
- violation of the right of citizens to protect their health from harmful information that is not realised by the individual;

- infringement of intellectual property;

б) for the community:

- obstacles in building an information society;
- deprivation of the right to the spiritual renewal of society, the preservation of its moral values, the affirmation in society of the ideals of high morality, patriotism and humanism, the development of the centuries-old spiritual traditions of the Fatherland, and the promotion of national and cultural heritage, norms of morality and public morality;
- manipulation of mass consciousness;
- creating an atmosphere that hinders the priority development of modern telecommunication technologies, preservation and development of domestic scientific and production potential;

в) for the state:

- counteraction:
- to protect the interests of the individual and society;
- to build the rule of law;
- formation of institutions of public control over public authorities;
- the formation of a system for the preparation, adoption and implementation of decisions by public authorities that balances the interests of the individual, society and the State;
- protection of state information systems and state information resources;
- defence of the country's unified information space.

The categories of information security violators can be grouped according to their qualifications: novice (adventurer), specialist (idea hacker, unreliable employee), professional (professional hacker). And if we match the motives of security breach and technical equipment of each group with these groups, we can get a generalised model of information security intruder, as shown in Fig. 3.1.

Figure 3.1. Information security intruder model.

The intruder model defines:

- categories of persons who may include the offender;
- possible targets of the intruder and their gradations in terms of importance and danger;
- assumptions about his qualifications;
- An assessment of its technical armoury;
- limitations and assumptions about the nature of his actions.

Guaranteed verification of the user's identity is the task of various identification and authentication mechanisms.

Each user (group of users) of the network is assigned a certain distinctive feature - an identifier and it is compared with the approved list. However, only the declared identifier in the network cannot provide protection against unauthorised connection without verifying the user's identity.

The process of verifying a user's identity is called authentication. It takes place with the help of a special distinctive characteristic presented by the user - authenticator, which is inherent to him. The effectiveness of authentication is determined, first of all, by the distinctive features of each user.

Specific identification and authentication mechanisms in the network can be implemented on the basis of the following information security tools and procedures:

- passwords;
- technical means;

- biometrics tools;
- cryptography with unique keys for each user.

Qualitative methods of risk management based on ISO 17999 requirements include COBRA and RA Software Tool. Let's briefly review these methodologies.

The COBRA methodology makes it possible to perform in an automated mode the simplest variant of information risk assessment for any company. For this purpose, it is proposed to use special electronic knowledge bases and logical inference procedures oriented to the requirements of ISO 17799. It is essential that, if desired, the list of requirements to be taken into account can be supplemented with various requirements of domestic regulatory bodies.

The COBRA methodology presents the requirements of ISO 17799 in the form of checklist's to be answered during the risk assessment of a company's information assets and electronic business transactions. The answers are then automatically processed and a final report with current assessments of the company's information risks and recommendations for their management is generated using the appropriate rules of logical inference.

The methodology and the RA Software Tool of the same name are based on the requirements of the international standards ISO 17999 and ISO 13335 (Parts 3 and 4), as well as on the requirements of some British National Standards Institute (BSI) guidelines, e.g. PD 3002 (Guidance on risk assessment and management), PD 3003 (Assessing a company's readiness for audit in accordance with BS 7799), PD 3005 (Guidance on selecting a protection system), etc. The methodology and the RA Software Tool of the same name are based on the requirements of the international standards ISO 17999 and ISO 13335 (Parts 3 and 4).

This methodology enables information risk assessment (modules 4 and 5) to be performed in accordance with the requirements of ISO 17799 and, if desired, in accordance with the more detailed specifications of the British Standards Institution's PD 3002 guidance.

The second group of risk management techniques are quantitative techniques, the relevance of which is due to the need to solve various optimisation problems that often arise in real life. The essence of these problems is reduced to the search for the only optimal solution out of many existing ones. For example, it is necessary to answer the following questions: "How, staying within the approved annual (quarterly) budget for information security, to achieve the maximum level of protection of information assets of the company?" or "Which of the alternatives for building corporate information security (secure WWW site or corporate Email) to choose, taking into account the known limitations of business resources of the company?". To solve these problems, methods and techniques of quantitative risk assessment and management are developed on the basis of structural and less often object-oriented methods of system analysis and design (SSADM - Structured Systems Analysis and Design). In practice, such risk management techniques allow:

- Create models of the company's information assets from a security perspective;
- Classify and assess the values of assets;
- Compile lists of the most significant security threats and vulnerabilities;
- Rank security threats and vulnerabilities;
- Justify risk controls and measures;
- Evaluate the effectiveness/cost of different defence options;
- Formalise and automate risk assessment and management procedures.

One of the best known techniques of this class is the CRAMM technique.

First, the CRAMM method was created, and then the CRAMM (risk analysis and control) methodology of the same name was created to meet the requirements of the CCTA. Then several versions of the methodology appeared, oriented to the requirements of various governmental and commercial organisations and structures. One of the "commercial profile" versions was widely spread in the information protection market.

The main objectives of the CRAMM methodology are:

- Formalisation and automation of risk analysis and management procedures;
- Optimise the cost of controls and security features;
- Comprehensive planning and risk management at all stages of the information systems lifecycle;
- Reduction of time for development and maintenance of the corporate information protection system;
- Justification of the effectiveness of the proposed protection measures and controls;

- Change and Incident Management;
- Business Continuity Support;
- Operational decision making on safety management issues, etc.

Risk management in the CRAMM methodology is carried out in several steps.

Figure 3.2: Stages of risk management in the CRAMM methodology.

At the first stage of initiation - "Initiation" - the boundaries of the company's information system under study, the composition and structure of its main information assets and transactions are defined.

The Identification and Valuation of Assets step clearly identifies assets and determines their value. The calculation of the value of information assets clearly identifies the need for and adequacy of the proposed controls and protections.

The Threat and Vulnerability Assessment stage identifies and assesses threats and vulnerabilities to the company's information assets.

The risk analysis stage - "Risk Analysis" - provides qualitative and quantitative risk assessments.

The risk management stage - Risk management - proposes measures and means to reduce or evade risk.

Let's consider the possibilities of CRAMM on the following example. Let's assume that information risks of the following corporate information system are being assessed.

Fig.3.3 CRAMM capabilities in corporate IS.

Risk management. The main steps of the risk management stage are presented in Figure 3.4.

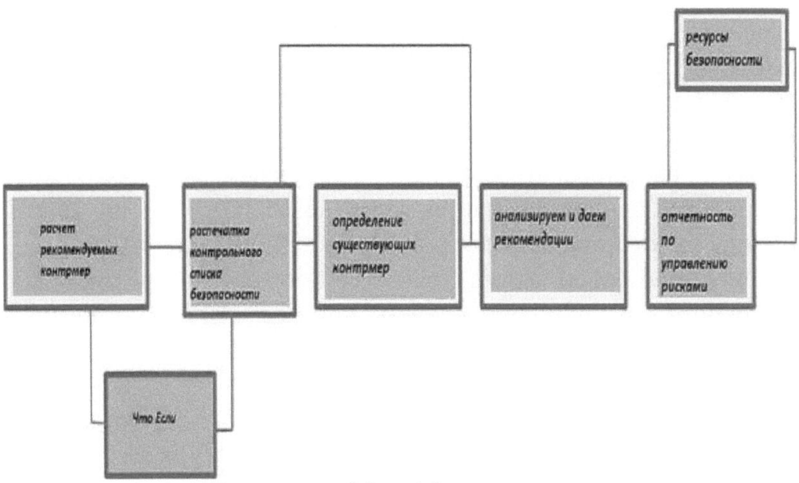

Fig.3.4 Key steps of the risk management stage.

At this stage, CRAMM generates several options for countermeasures adequate to the identified risks and their levels. Countermeasures are categorised into groups and subgroups according to the following categories:

- Ensuring security at the network level.
- Ensuring physical security.

- Ensuring the security of the supporting infrastructure.
- Security measures at the system administrator level.

§3.2 Selecting priority factors for a conceptual model of state information security

The new stage in the development of information exchange, which is characterised by the intensive introduction of modern information technologies, widespread use of local, corporate and global networks in all spheres of life of a civilised state, creates new opportunities and quality of information exchange. In this regard, the problems of information security (IS) are of paramount importance, the relevance and importance of which is due to the following factors:

- high growth rates of the fleet of personal computers (PCs) used in various spheres of activity and, as a consequence, a sharp expansion of the range of users with direct access to computing networks and information resources;
- increase in the amount of information accumulated, stored and processed using PCs and other means of automation;
- rapid development of hardware and software and technologies that do not meet modern security requirements;
- inconsistency between the rapid development of information processing tools and IS theory development of international standards and legal norms ensuring the necessary level of information protection (IP);
- ubiquitous spread of network technologies, creation of a unified information and communication world space based on the Internet, which by its ideology does not provide a sufficient level of IS.

The above-mentioned factors create a certain spectrum of IS threats at the level of an individual, society and the state. The means of neutralising a significant part of them is the formation of IS theory and information protection methodology.

Information as an indispensable component of any organised system is, on the one hand, easily vulnerable (i.e. it is very accessible to the destabilising effects of a large number of diverse threats), and, on the other hand, can itself be a source of a large number of diverse threats, both for the elements of the system itself and for the external environment. Hence, ensuring information security in the general formulation of the problem can be achieved only with the interconnected solution of the three constituent problems:

- protection of information in the system from destabilising effects of external and internal threats to information;

- protection of system elements from destabilising effects of external and internal information threats;
- protection of the external environment from information threats from the system in question.

In accordance with the above, the conceptual model of information security can be represented as shown in Fig. 3.5.

It should be noted that the problem of protection against information is significantly more complex than the problem of information protection due to the diversity of information threats, the impact of which is not always obvious. The prevention and neutralisation of such threats require both technical solutions and organisational, legal and political solutions at the domestic, intergovernmental and international levels.

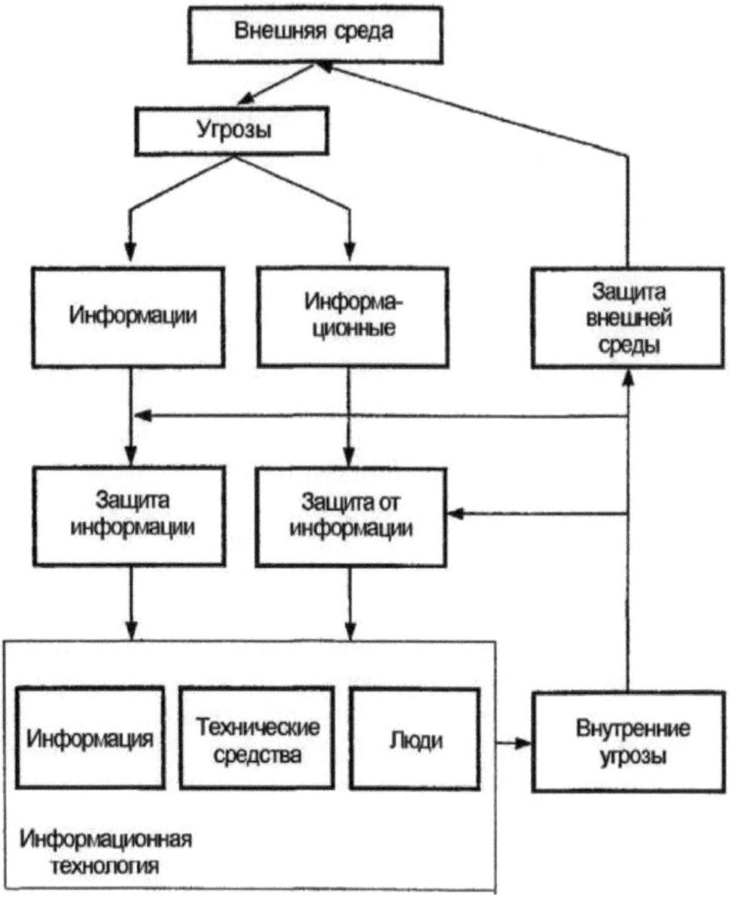

Fig.3.5. Conceptual model of information security provision.

At the present stage of society development the role of the information sphere, which is a set of information, information infrastructure, subjects that collect, form, disseminate and use information, as well as the system of regulation of public relations arising in this process, is increasing.

The information sphere as a system-forming factor of society actively influences the state of political, economic, defence and other security components of the RUz, the national security of the RUz depends significantly on ensuring information security, and in the course of technological progress this dependence will increase.

Normal vital activity of the social organism is determined by the level of development, quality of functioning and security of the information environment. Production and management, defence and communications, transport and energy, finance, science and education, mass media - everything depends on the intensity of information exchange, completeness, timeliness and reliability of information. It is the information infrastructure of society that is the target of information weapons. But, first of all, the new weapon is aimed at the armed forces, enterprises of the defence complex, structures responsible for external and internal security of the country. The high degree of state management structures of the domestic economy can lead to disastrous consequences as a result of information aggression. The rate of improvement of information weapons exceeds the rate of development of defence technologies. Therefore, the task of neutralisation of information weapons, reflection of the threat of their use should be considered as a priority in ensuring the national security of the country.

The destruction of certain types of consciousness presupposes the destruction and reorganisation of the communities that constitute this type of consciousness.

Five main ways of defeating and destroying consciousness in consciential warfare are distinguished:

- lesion of the neurocerebral substrate, reducing the level of functioning of consciousness, which can occur under the influence of chemicals, prolonged poisoning of air, food, radiation;
- lowering the level of organisation of the information and communication environment on the basis of its disintegration and

primitivisation, in which consciousness functions;
- occult influence on the organisation of consciousness on the basis of directed transmission of thought-forms to the subject of defeat;
- special organisation and dissemination through communication channels of images and texts that destroy the workings of consciousness (psychotronic weapons);
- destruction of the ways and forms of personal identification in relation to fixed communities, leading to a change of forms of self-determination and depersonalisation.

The impact of changing and transforming the types of imindji-dentifications (deep identification with a particular position represented by a particular image) and authentisations (feelings of personal authenticity) is carried out by the mass media, primarily television.

The ultimate goal of the use of conscientisation weapons is the removal of people from the established forms of megacommunities. The destruction of the people and their transformation into a population occurs due to the fact that no one wants to associate and relate themselves with the polyethnos to which they previously belonged. The destruction of identifications is aimed at destroying the mechanisms of a person's inclusion in naturally formed and existing communities and replacing these evolutionary-naturally formed communities with one completely artificial one - the community of viewers around the TV set. It does not matter how a person feels about what he sees and hears from the TV screen, it is important that he should be a regular viewer. In this case, he can be influenced in a targeted and sustainable way. In conditions of formal peace and so-called local wars, conscientious warfare is very effective.

Thus, the problem of global counteraction to threats to information security is aggravated by the fact that there is still no universally accepted definition of "information weapons". Complicating this issue is the fact that information technologies are mostly non-military or dual-use technologies. Information aggressions can be carried out with the help of ordinary personal computers using the extensive technological capabilities of the Internet, and there are numerous examples of this.

The problem of ensuring international information security is also complicated by the fact that it has not yet become an object of regulation of international law. In the era of globalisation, which has affected both the scientific, technological and information and telecommunication spheres, communications between countries are becoming increasingly dependent on information technology-based infrastructures that cross national borders. The international nature of the threats of information aggression and crime necessitates co-operation at both the regional and global levels in order to take concerted action to reduce existing threats. No State can achieve this alone.

Awareness of the fact that the emergence and spread of information weapons and militarisation of information technologies is a powerful destabilising factor in international relations makes it necessary for the UN to be an organisation capable of providing a comprehensive solution to any political problem, with the widest possible representation and maximum consideration of the interests of the entire world community.

The value of information changes over time. As a rule, the value of information decreases with time. Dependence of information value on time is approximated according to the expression:

$$C(t) = C_0 e^{-2,3t/\tau} \qquad (3.1)$$

where C_0 - value of information at the moment of its origin (receipt); t - time from the moment of origin of information to the moment of its value determination; т - time from the moment of origin of information to the moment of its obsolescence.

The time after which information becomes obsolete varies over a very wide range. For example, for jet pilots and car racers, information about the position of cars in space becomes obsolete in a fraction of a second. At the same time, information about the laws of nature remains relevant for many centuries.

The following approaches are used to measure the quantity of information.

A. An entropy approach.

In information theory, the amount of information is measured by the measure of the reduction in the recipient's uncertainty (entropy) in choosing or waiting for events after receiving the information. The amount of information is greater the lower the probability of an event. The entropy approach is widely used in determining the amount of information transmitted through communication channels. The choice when receiving information is made between alphabetical characters in the received message.

Shannon K., using the methodology of R. Hartley, drew attention to the fact that when transmitting verbal messages, the frequency of use of different letters of the alphabet is not equal: some letters are used very often, others rarely. There is also a certain correlation in letter sequences, when the occurrence of one of the letters is very likely to be followed by a particular other letter. By introducing these probability values p into R. Hartley's formula, K. Shannon obtained new expressions for determining the amount of information. For one symbol this expression takes the form:

$$H = -p\log_2 p, \qquad (3.2)$$

and a message consisting of "n" characters:

$$H = -\sum_{i=1}^{n} p_i \log_2 p_i \qquad (3.3)$$

The expression (3.3), repeating in form the expression for entropy in statistical mechanics, was called entropy by K. Shannon by analogy.

This approach fundamentally changed the concept of information. Information is now understood not as any messages transmitted in a communication system, but only those that reduce the uncertainty of the recipient of information about the object, and the more this uncertainty is reduced, i.e. the more the entropy of the message is reduced, the higher the informativeness of the received message. Entropy is the minimum information that must be obtained to eliminate the uncertainty of the alphabet used by the source of information.

An analysis of Shannon's formula shows that the amount of information in binary representation (in bits or bytes) depends on two quantities: the number of characters in the message and the frequency of occurrence of this or that character in messages for the alphabet used. This approach does not reflect at all how useful the received information is, and allows to determine only the cost of message transmission.

Б. The thesaurus approach.

This approach is proposed by Y.A. Shrader. It is based on the consideration of information as knowledge. According to this approach, the amount of information extracted by a person from a message can be estimated by the degree of change in his/her knowledge. Structured knowledge represented in the form of concepts and relations between them is called thesaurus. The structure of the thesaurus is hierarchical. Concepts and relations, grouped together, form other, more complex concepts and relations.

Knowledge of an individual person, organisation, state form corresponding thesauri. Thesauri of organisational structures form thesauri of their constituent elements. Thus, the thesaurus of an organisation is formed, first of all, by thesauri of employees, as well as other information carriers, such as documents, equipment, products, etc. Knowledge transfer requires that the thesauri of the transmitting and receiving elements overlap. Otherwise the thesaurus owners will not understand each other.

Thesauri of a person and any organisational structures are their capital. Therefore, thesaurus owners strive to maintain and increase their thesaurus. Increasing the thesaurus is done through training, buying a licence, inviting qualified employees or stealing information.

Two tendencies are observed in society: development of thesauri of individual elements (people, organised structures) and alignment of thesauri of elements of society. Thesaurus alignment occurs both as a result of purposeful activity (e.g., training) and spontaneously. Spontaneous alignment of thesauri occurs due to accidental transfer of knowledge, including illegal transfer.

Understanding information security as "the state of protection of the information environment of society, ensuring its formation, use and development in the interests of citizens and organisations", it is legitimate to identify threats to information security, sources of these threats, ways of their implementation and goals, as well as other conditions and actions that violate security. At the same time, of course, it is necessary to consider measures to protect information from unlawful actions leading to damage.

Practice has shown that in order to analyse such a significant set of sources, objects and actions, it is advisable to use modelling methods that create a "substitute" of real situations. It should be taken into account that the model does not copy the original, it is simpler. The model should be general enough to describe real actions taking into account their complexity.

In generalised form, the considered components in the form of a conceptual model of information security are shown in the following scheme (Fig.3.6.).

The main elements of the conceptual model are discussed in more detail in Annex 2.

The analysis of the current state of information security in RUz shows that the level of information security currently does not meet the vital needs of the individual, society and the state.

Today's conditions of political and socio-economic development of the country cause the aggravation of contradictions between the needs of society in expanding the free exchange of information and the need to maintain certain restrictions on its dissemination.

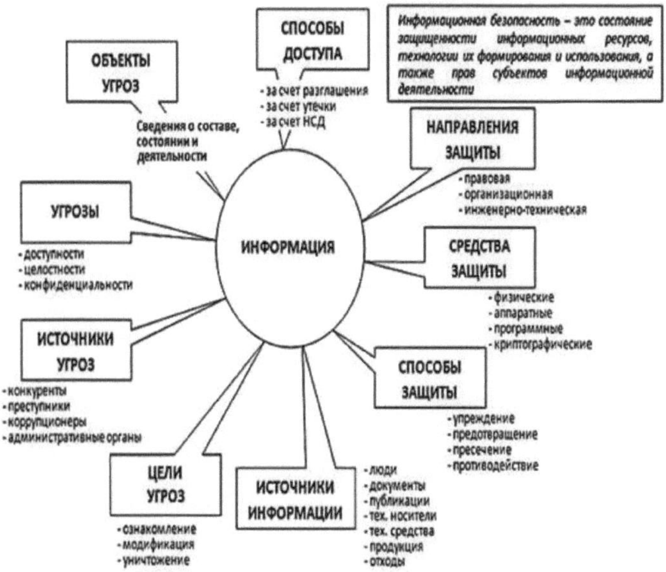

Fig.3.6. Conceptual model of information security

The lack of effective mechanisms for regulating information relations in society and the state leads to many negative consequences.

Weak provision of state authorities and management bodies with complete, reliable and timely information makes it difficult to make informed decisions. Underdevelopment of information relations in the sphere of entrepreneurship hinders the formation of a civilised market. The lack of a mechanism for inclusion of information resources in the economic turnover leads to serious economic losses.

Insufficient protection of the state information resource leads to the loss of important political, economic and scientific-technical information, including on new and highly effective technologies of military and dual-purpose.

Failure to ensure citizens' rights to information, manipulation of information causes inadequate reaction of the population and in some

cases leads to political instability in society.
Losses of important information are facilitated by haphazard data protection and poor coordination of information protection measures on a national scale, departmental disunity in ensuring the integrity and confidentiality of "information, weak control over the export of domestic science-intensive technologies, weapons and military equipment.
The situation with the protection of state secrets is unfavourable. Measures to ensure the protection of State secrets, commercial and official secrets have been seriously weakened in State and administrative bodies and defence enterprises.
Of the external sources of threats, the following are most capable of affecting the information security of defence facilities:
all types of intelligence activities of foreign states;
information-technical impacts (electronic warfare methods, penetration of computer networks, etc.) on the part of probable adversaries;
psychological operations of probable adversaries, carried out by special methods and through the activities of the mass media;
activities of foreign political and economic structures directed against the interests of the RUz in the defence sphere.
The main directions of ensuring information security in nationwide information and telecommunication systems are:
prevention of interception by technical means of information transmitted through communication channels;
exclusion of unauthorised access to information processed or stored in technical means;
prevention of leakage of processed information due to side electromagnetic emissions and interference created by functioning technical means, as well as electroacoustic transformations;
prevention of special software and hardware effects causing destruction, destruction, distortion of information or malfunctions of informatisation means;
Identification of electronic interception devices (pawning devices) embedded in facilities and technical means;
prevention of interception of speech information from premises and objects by technical means.
Preventing the interception by technical means of information transmitted through communication channels is achieved through the

use of cryptographic and other methods and means of protection, as well as through organisational, technical and security measures.

§3.3 Methods of building a conceptual model of state information security

The information description of the object in the form of a set of parameters as a generalised control system is presented in Fig. 1, which includes input influences on the object X, the characteristic of its state at the output - Y and the control action - U, formed by the control device on the basis of the incoming information about the state of the object at the input - Ix and output - Iy, about the control objectives - Iz, as well as about the environment of the object - the external environment - Is.

All objects, different in essence, can be represented in the form of one universal model, which uses an informational description of the object. Thus, all information about an object can be represented in the form of a set of versatile parameters or indicators that characterise its state and behaviour in time.

Fig. 3.7.Generalised information description of the object

In this case, the vector $Y=(Y_1, Y_2, ..., Y_n)$ represents the output or controllable parameters. It is these parameters that inform about what state the object is in and how it meets the control objectives.

Vector $X=(X_1, x2, ..., X_r)$ defines the input, or setting (controlled), parameters that are the cause of changes in the state of the object.

Vector $U=(U_1, U_2, ..., U_M)$ denotes the parameters of perturbing control actions on the object according to the adopted control objective and its algorithm.

The vector F = (Fl,F2, ...,Fk) shows the pair metres of perturbing uncontrolled and uncontrollable influences, which are a consequence of the influence of external environmental factors or other internal factors.

These parameters reflect disturbances in the control. If a parameter of this kind can be controlled, then this parameter is transferred to the group of input parameters, i.e. it is included in the x vector.

In the general case, the vector Y is a nonlinear vector function of the setting, control and external influences:

$$Y = Y\ (X, U, F). \qquad (3.4)$$

The coordinates of vectors u and y are called control and controlled coordinates, respectively. If the control object is characterised by one control and one controlled quantity, i.e. vectors U and Y have one coordinate each, the object is called simple, one-dimensional or single-linked. If the vectors U and Y have several coordinates, the object is called multidimensional. If there are several mutually related coordinates of vectors U and Y, the object is called multilinked.

Information about the control objectives is embedded in the control algorithm, which can be represented as a functional dependence

$$U(t) = F\ (y, x, f), \qquad (3.5)$$

where F is some generally nonlinear vector function of the controlled parameters y, setting parameters x and perturbing influences f.

The term "signalling information" covers quite a wide variety of possible schemes of information communication existing in practice. This is, in particular, visual (video) observation of the situation, alphanumeric information in the form of documents (physical or in the form of signals), graphic or drawing materials, symbolic-digital on various carriers and even in the form of physical samples of materials, products and so on.

In this regard, it is necessary to further split the concept of signalling information by species. Let us distinguish two varieties: analogue-digital and volumetric-species. Knowledge of the physical form of information manifestation in a particular information threat scenario is theoretically sufficient to compare homogeneous information threats within the same environment or protection zone Fig. 3.8.

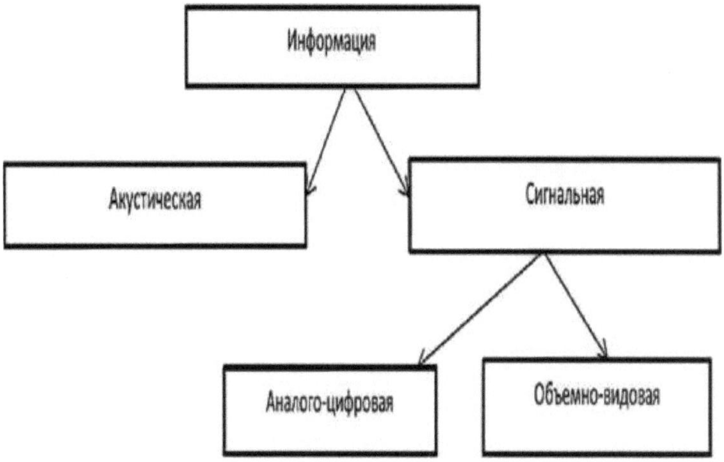

Fig. 3.8. Scheme of information classification by physical form of manifestation.

However, this knowledge is not sufficient to compare the threats and possible damage from them for different conditions or different protection zones. It is necessary to classify information according to its importance. The importance of information is set by its owners in some discrete scale of categories Fig.3.9.

Fig.3.9. Properties of information.

Let us consider a geometric model of a protection system. Let $P = (p\ p_{1,\ 2}\ , ..., p_z)$ *be the* set of defences, and $A = (a_1\ a_2\ , ..., a_n)$ *be the* set of attacks. Those attacks that cannot be expressed by combinations of attacks are called independent attacks. Their set *A'* is a subset of

the set A - the basis of attacks. Let us choose the space Rn, pa3Mep- nity of which coincides with the power of the set A, for the construction of the geometric model of the NWI.
Any A/bA attack is matched by certain defences $(p'_1, p'_2,..., p'_k) \subset P$.
Let us denote this set $\{p'_1, p'_2,..., p'_l\} = P_{ri}$.
If the means P_j ·, does not belong to the set P_{ri}, then the attack A,is not dangerous for it.
The coordinate axes in space ^ represent threat classes. The unit of measurement on the coordinate axes is an independent attack to which a defence is assigned. For each attack, the coordinate values of the corresponding vector indicate the defences included in the system under study.
As an example, let's consider the attack "Unauthorised access to information stored on a workstation by an external intruder" in Cartesian space, where the x-axis is threats related to physical protection; y- threats related to hardware and software protection; z- threats related to organisational and legal protection. An attack can be realised if three protection measures are not met: "Intruder in controlled area", "Unlocked OS session" and "Security breach".

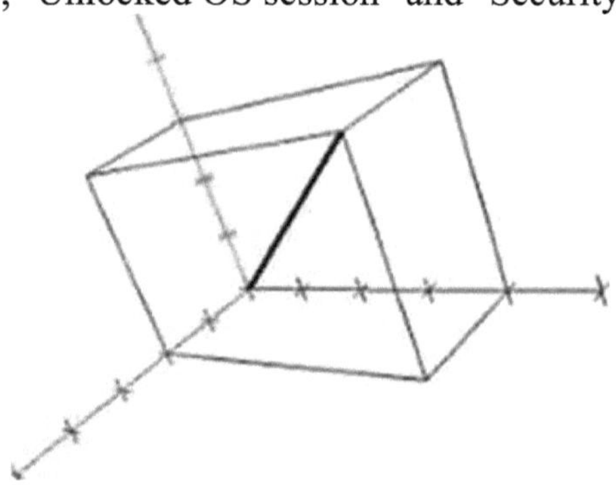

Fig. 3.10.Attack model "Unauthorised access to information stored on the workstation by an external intruder".

This attack can be realised in other ways, such as "Connection to the technical means and systems of OM", "Use of bookmarking means", "Disguise as a registered user", "Software defects and vulnerabilities", "Introduction of software bookmarks", "Use of viruses and other malicious software code", "Theft of protected information media", "Disruption of information processing TCs" (Fig.3.11).
Initially, each vector Pi, is in the first coordinate octant. Let us

construct in R^n the surface of a convex polyhedron S such that each of its vertices coincides with the end of one of the vectors p1, p2, ..., pz. The surface of the polyhedron S together with vectors p1, p2, ..., pz will be considered as a geometric model of NWI.

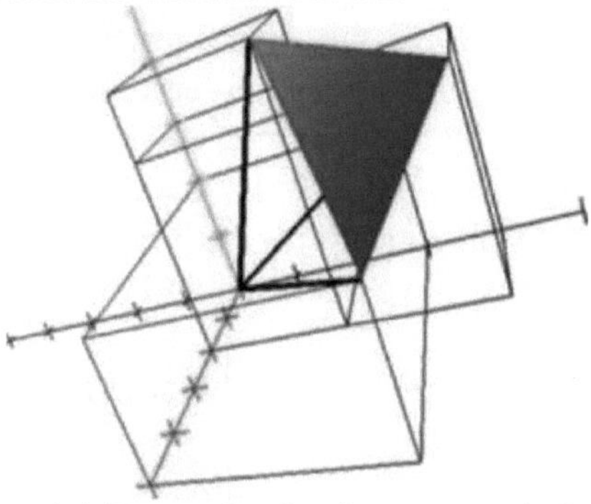

Fig.3.11. Attack model "Unauthorised access to information stored on the workstation by an external intruder"

The effect of any attack A_t is naturally formalised by the reflection of a vector along the axis with an unfulfilled defence measure. Thanks to this way of modelling, the vectors corresponding to the means for which this attack is not dangerous will not change their position.
So, only the i-th coordinate of p1 vectors will change after the impact of the attack A_i in the proposed modelling method,
p_2, ..., p_z entering the geometric model, and all other coordinates will remain unchanged.
Based on the results of attack modelling, it is possible to judge the sensitivity or insensitivity of the information system (IS) to disturbing influences. If the coordinates of the polyhedron belong to the first coordinate octant, it is concluded that the IS is insensitive to the disturbing influence, otherwise it is concluded that the protective measures are insufficient. The measure of stability is reduced to the number of iterations at which the IC remains undisturbed to the effects of combinations of attacks.
The primary list of threats is formed by combinations of all possible factors affecting the protected information, categories of protection means and levels of intruders' impact (Fig. 3.11).
Identification and consideration of factors that affect or may affect the protected information in specific conditions form the basis for planning and carrying out effective measures to ensure information protection at the object of informatisation. Completeness and

reliability of identification of factors is achieved by considering the full set of factors affecting all elements of the object of informatisation at all stages of information processing.

Threats of information leakage through technical channels are unambiguously described by the characteristics of the information source, propagation medium and receiver of the informative signal, i.e. they are determined by the characteristics of the technical channel of information leakage.

The secondary list of threats is created by adding to it based on statistics on incidents that have occurred and on the conditional degree of their destructive impact.

The degree of perturbing influence can be determined:

- the likelihood of a threat;
- the loss from the realisation of the threat;
- the system's recovery time.

The considered methodology of building a threat model allows to solve the problems of developing private models of information security threats in specific systems, taking into account their purpose, conditions and features of functioning. The purpose of such modelling is to control the level of IS security by risk analysis methods and to develop an effective information protection system that ensures neutralisation of the anticipated threats.

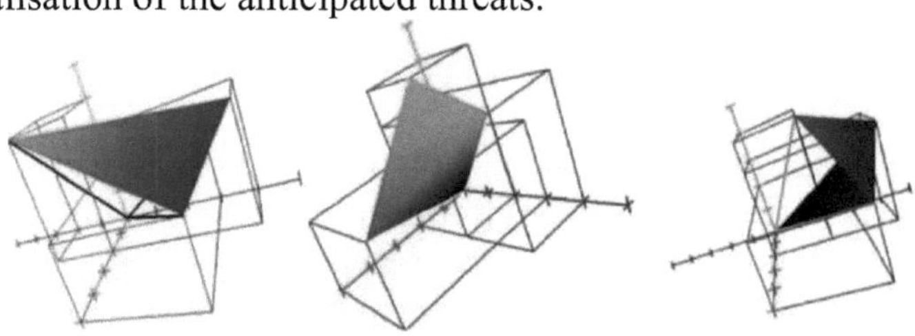

Fig.3.12. Modelling results

One of the main tasks of ensuring information security in ACS of critical facilities is to determine the list of threats to information security with the assessment of risks of impact of actual threats on the protected ACS ACS ACS ACS. The solution of these tasks makes it possible to determine the requirements to the system of protection of ASU KVO, to form a list of protective measures and, as a result, to determine the optimal structure of the system of protection of ASU KVO from various types of information and technical impacts.

The process of assessing threats to information security and forming a list of threats relevant to the protected ACS of the IED is called information security threat modelling, and the result of this process is a threat model, which is a physical, mathematical or descriptive representation of the properties or characteristics of information security threats.

An algorithm for building an ER model of the threat model database in Chen's notation is given in Appendix 1.

The purpose of information security threat modelling is to define a system of specific requirements for information protection in the ASU KVO, ensuring its safe operation, and to create an adequate system of information protection in the ASU KVO based on these requirements (Fig. 3.13).

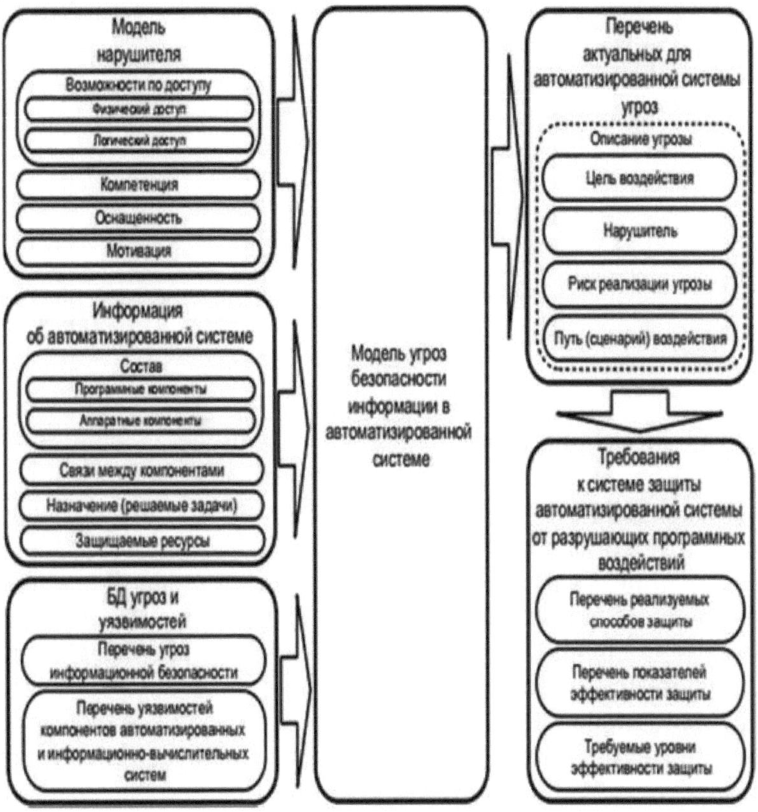

Fig.3.13. The process of modelling information security threats in ACS KVO.

The result of modelling an information security intruder is its model, which is included in the security threat model of the ACS KVO as one of its components (Fig.3.14) and contains:

- physical access level (PhL) to the information and (or) to the components of the ACS KVO;
- logical access level (LogL) to the information and (or) to the components of the ACS KVO;
- the level of competence (C) of the information security intruder;
- the level of equipment (A) of the information security intruder;
- motivation (M) of the information security violator.

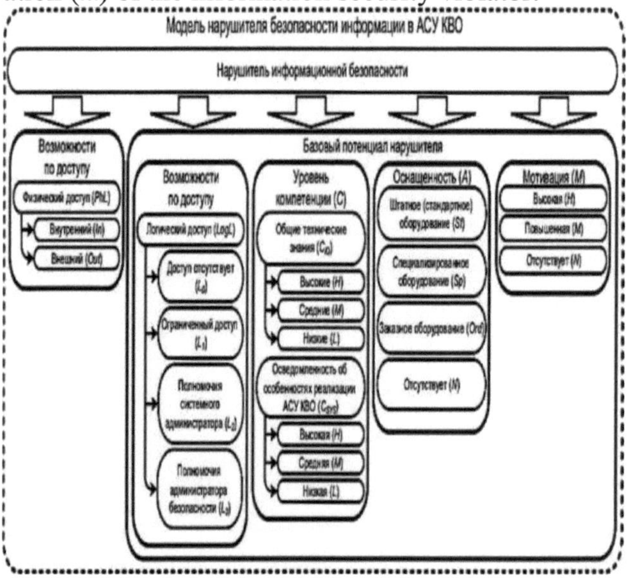

Fig.3.14. Model of the information security intruder in the ACS KVO.

A general record of the intruder model is made as a string PhL:[x]/LogL:[x]/C:[x]/A:[x]/M:[x], where the value of the corresponding parameter is written instead of [x].

The level of physical access is determined based on the availability of physical access to information and (or) components of the ASU KVO. With this in mind, we can distinguish two levels of information security violators in the ASU KVO:

- internal intruders (In) - persons who have the ability to access the information system or its individual components on a permanent or ad hoc basis;
- external intruders (Out) - persons who do not have access to the information system or its separate parts and who realise threats to information security remotely (remotely), being outside the information system.

The level of logical access is determined taking into account the access rights of subjects (individuals) to the objects of the ACS KVO. Based on this, the following levels of logical access can be distinguished:

- persons who do not have access to the ACS objects (L_0);
- registered users of the ASU KVO having limited access to the ASU KVO objects from the automated workplace (L_1);
- registered users of the IES ACS having access to the IES ACS objects with the authorisation of the IES ACS system administrator (L_2);
- registered users of the ASCE ACS who have access to the ASCE ACS objects with the ASCE ACS security administrator's authorisation (L_3).

The level of competence of the information security intruder is determined on the basis of assumptions about the general technical knowledge of the intruder and his awareness of the peculiarities of the construction and operation of the attacked ASIC, as well as the specifics of its operation.

An intruder's general technical knowledge (CIQ) is assessed by three levels:

- high - the perpetrator has a high awareness of methods and means of information protection applied in various information systems, as well as knowledge of methods of identifying vulnerabilities and realisation of security threats in various automated systems;
- medium - the intruder is aware of the methods and means of information protection used in various automated systems;
- low - the perpetrator has a weak awareness of methods and means of information protection applied in various information systems and has no knowledge of the realisation of security threats.

Each of the above-mentioned levels of general technical knowledge is assigned a numerical value. Thus, the numerical values of the characteristics of the levels of general technical knowledge of the ACS KVO information security intruder are as follows: high level - 5, medium level - 2, low level - 0.

The intruder's awareness of the peculiarities of the construction and operation of the CSYS under attack is also assessed by three levels:

- high - the intruder is able to gain access to information about the structure and functional links in the ASU KVO, the information protection system in the ASU KVO, as well as to information from design, engineering and operational documentation;

- medium - the intruder is able to gain access to information about the goals and objectives of the ASU KVO, as well as to information from the operational documentation;
- low - the intruder cannot gain access to information about the structure and functional links in the ASU KVO, the information protection system in the ASU KVO, as well as to information from design, engineering and operational documentation.

A numerical value is assigned to each of the above-mentioned levels of the intruder's awareness of the specifics of the implementation of the attacked ASIC. Thus, the numerical values of the characteristics of the intruder's awareness levels of the specifics of implementing the attacked ASIC are as follows: high level - 5, medium level - 2, low level - 0.

The general level of competence (C) of an information security intruder in the ASU of the IACS is estimated based on the sum of the numerical values of CIQ and CSYS as follows:

high *(H)* when (CIQ + CSYS) >5,

C = mean (M) at 2 <(CIQ +CSYS)≤ 5, (3.6)

low (L) when (CIQ + CSYS) ≤ 2.

Motivation is a valid factor in an intruder's potential, which can be used to describe various aspects related to the intruder as well as to the resources of the IED ASA of interest to the intruder. Motivation can imply a certain probability of attack: a threat assessed as highly motivated may suggest that an attack on the IED ASA is imminent or that an attack is not expected due to an unmotivated threat.

In general, the motivation of an information security intruder in the ACS KVO can be assessed by three levels:

- high (H) - there is information about intruders' intentions to a specific information system, its separate components or there is information received from executive authorities about intruder's intentions to carry out illegal actions with regard to the ASU KVO or information contained in it;
- elevated (M) - the offender acts out of any personal motives (curiosity, desire to assert oneself, etc.);
- absent (N) - information security breaches occur due to unintentional, careless (erroneous) or unqualified actions.

The intruder's equipment characterises the possibility of his access to software and (or) hardware-software means, which he can use when implementing security threats in the ASU KVO:

- standard (standard) equipment (St) - software and (or) hardware and software tools that are easily accessible to an intruder (these tools may be part of the ASU KVO itself, and may also be easily obtained, such as, for example, known and available software that can be downloaded from the Internet);
- specialised equipment (Sp) - software and (or) hardware and software tools that are limitedly available to an infringer, but which he can acquire without significant effort;
- custom equipment (Ord) - software and (or) hardware and software tools that are not available to the general public because either special development may be required, or the distribution of these tools is controlled and limited, or these tools have a very high cost;
- No (N) - the intruder does not have access to any software and (or) hardware and software.

The intruder's ability to logically access the system components, his competence and equipment level, as well as his motivation determine the basic potential (PtBASE) possessed by an intruder of information security in the ASU KVO and used at the stage of threat modelling when assessing the probabilities of their implementation. The preliminary basic potential of the intruder is estimated on the basis of numerical values of competence and equipment levels in accordance with Table 3.1.

Table 3.1.

Numerical values of the characteristics of the intruder's competence levels and his equipment

Level	Indicator of the offender's capabilities	Numerical Characteristic value
Level of competence (C	low	0
	average	2
	high	5
Level of equipment *(A)*	absent	0
	standard equipment	1
	specialised equipment	3
	customised equipment	5

The values obtained from Table 1 are summed and the preliminary intruder baseline potential is determined:

$$Pt_{BASE} = \begin{cases} \text{высокий (H) при } (C + A) \geq 8, \\ \text{средний (M) при } 5 \leq (C + A) < 8, \\ \text{низкий (L) при } 3 \leq (C + A) < 5, \end{cases} \quad (3.7)$$

high (H) with $(C + A) \geq 8$,
Pt BASE = *c* mean (M) at $5 \leq (C + A) < 8$,
low (L) at $3 \leq (C + A) < 5$, <
is absent (N) when $(C + A) < 3$.

In case of high motivation, the intruder's potential goes to the next level (from low to medium or from medium to high), in case of lack of motivation, the potential goes from medium or high to low. In case the intruder has no possibilities for threat realisation (the basic potential has the level "absent"), regardless of the intruder's motivation, the basic potential remains at the level "absent".

Examples of description of different categories of intruders in accordance with the proposed model of information security intruder in ACS KVO are given in Table 3.2.

Table 3.2.

Examples of description of different categories of information security violators in the ACS KVO

Category of offender	Motive for the offender's actions	General record of the intruder model	Basic capacity
Intelligence services of foreign States	Damage to the state, certain spheres of its activity or sectors of the economy	*PhL:Out/LogL:Lo/C:H/A:Ord/M:H*	high
Developers, manufacturers and suppliers of KBO ACS components	Causing property damage by deceit or breach of trust	*PhL:Out/LogL:Li/C:H/A:Sp/M:M*	high
KBO automated control system operator	Unintentional, negligent or unqualified acts	*PhL:In/LogL:L\/C:/A:St/M:N*	low
Administrator of ACS KBO	Curiosity or desire for fulfilment	*PhL:In/LogL:L2/C:H/A:St/M:M*	high

When modelling information security threats in the ASU KVO, it is necessary to take into account its structure, including the presence of levels (segments), tasks to be solved, composition, physical, logical, functional and technological interconnections, interaction with other automated (information) systems and information and telecommunication networks, modes of operation of the ASU KVO, as well as the criticality of resources (information and components of the ASU KVO) to be protected.

The simplest and most illustrative way of modelling and describing possible scenarios of information security threat implementation is the application of attack tree apparatus.

Attack trees are quite a powerful and flexible tool for solving a multitude of security-related problems, including correlation and prevention of, and response to, impacts to information.

Attack trees, due to their graph structure, visually represent variants of information-technical impact on the automated system and, by analogy with a fault tree, are an organised graphical representation of conditions or other factors causing an undesirable event, called an event node.

For each possible threat and intruder for a particular ASIC, an attack tree is built. The top of this tree is the realisation of an information security threat. To reach the top of the tree, an information security intruder needs to fulfil a certain number of conditions at different levels of the ASIC, which will be intermediate vertices of the attack tree. Fig.3.15 shows an example of a two-level attack tree for the threat of information spoofing from field-level sensors (based on the multi-level structure of the ASU KVO), which shows that the threat will be realised if the intruder manages to fulfil at least one of the conditions of the second level ("OR-decomposition" of the information security threat).

Similarly, an "AND-decomposition" can be depicted to ensure that the goal can be achieved when all conditions at the lowest level of the tree are met simultaneously, and

"OR-NO decomposition" in which the goal can be achieved if only one of the conditions at the lowest level is fulfilled.

Security threat scenarios are all possible paths from the lowest level elements to the final target at the first level of the attack tree. For example, for the attack tree shown in Fig. 3.14, one of the scenarios of realisation of the threat of information spoofing from field level sensors will be the following path:

T 3.1→T 2.1→T 1.

The main problem of building attack trees is scalability, i.e. the possibility of building attack trees for information or automated systems that have a complex structure with a large number of

components and links between them with a high level of detail (i.e. the lowest level of the attack tree will reflect conditions that are not subject to further detail).
In order to reduce the complexity of analysis and the time required to build attack trees for IED ACSs that have a complex structure and a large number of components, it is necessary to drill down to a lower level only for actual threat scenarios.

Fig.3.15. An example of a two-level attack tree.
Modelling of information security breach processes is advisable based on the consideration of the logical chain: "threat - threat source - method of implementation - vulnerability - consequences" (Fig. 3.16.).
Threats are categorised according to the possibility of damage to the subject of the relationship when security objectives are violated. The damage can be caused by a subject (crime, fault or negligence), as well as a consequence of manifestations beyond the subject's control. There are not many threats.
Classification of possibilities of threat realisation, i.e. attacks, is a set of possible variants of actions of the source of threats by certain methods of realisation with the use of vulnerabilities that lead to the realisation of
of the attack targets are given in Appendix 2.

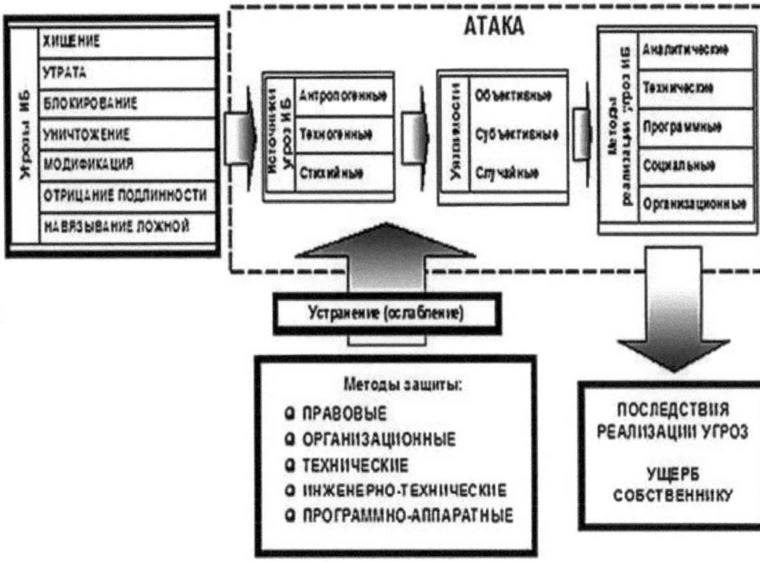

Fig.3.16. IS threat realisation model

The goal of the attack may not coincide with the goal of threat realisation and may be aimed at obtaining an intermediate result necessary to achieve further realisation of the threat. In the case of non-coincidence of the purpose of the attack with the goal of threat realisation, the attack itself is considered as a stage of preparation for the commission of actions aimed at the realisation of the threat, i.e. as "preparation for the commission" of an illegal action.

The result of an attack is the consequences that are the realisation of the threat and/or contribute to such realisation.

The very approach to analysing and assessing the state of information security is based on the calculation of weighted hazard coefficients for sources of threats and vulnerabilities, comparison of these coefficients with a predetermined criterion and consistent reduction (exclusion) of the full list of possible sources of threats and vulnerabilities to the minimum relevant for a particular object.

The results of the assessment and analysis can be used in the selection of adequate optimal methods of parrying threats, as well as in the audit of the real state of information security of the object for the purposes of its insurance.

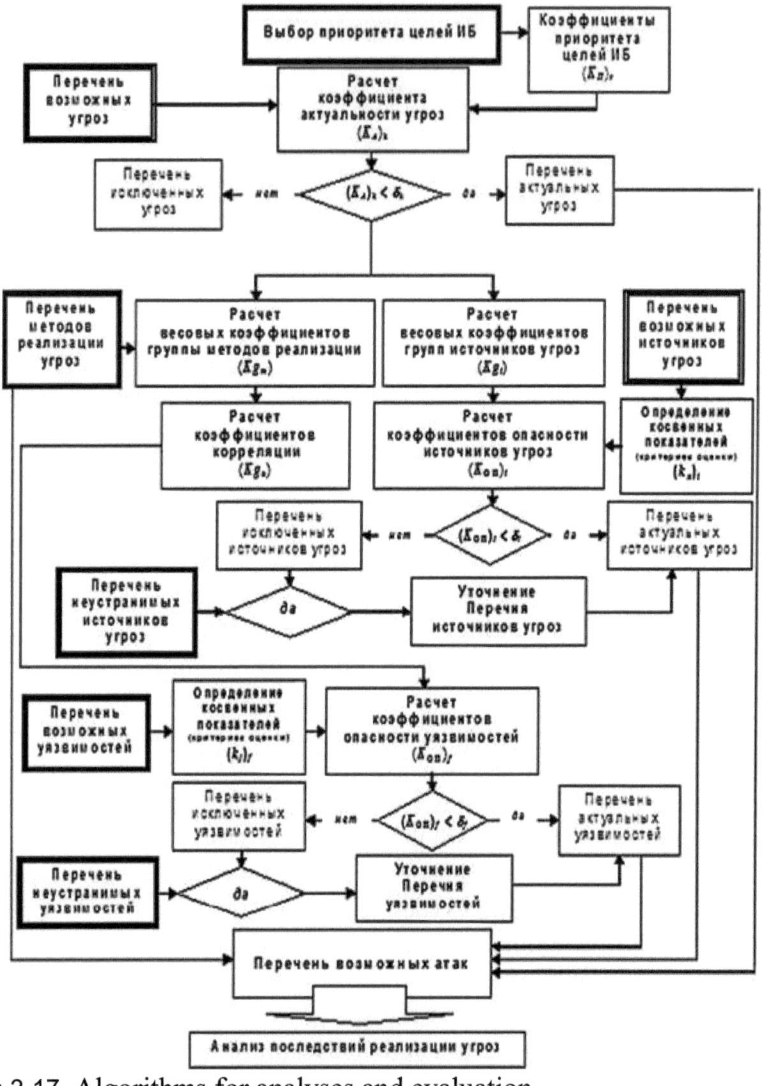

Fig.3.17. Algorithms for analyses and evaluation

Having described the composition of information security threats, we have not yet solved the problem of modelling their impact. All these threats manifest themselves differently at each point of the corporate network. Therefore, let us try to estimate, based on the usual logic, at which point which threat poses the greatest danger. Overlaying the information security threats on the corporate network model allows us to estimate them in the first approximation (Fig. 3.17).

Effective implementation, maintenance and development of a set of protection measures are possible only if there is a formalised system approach to information security.

§3.4 Algorithms for regulating the strategy of interstate relations on the basis of digital diplomacy

Digital diplomacy aims to carry out foreign policy information tasks with the help of various communicative practices in a new context of reality for this subject area. The need to study such communication is connected with a number of factors, in particular: the increase in information flows, the inclusion of diplomatic communication in the global context of speech interaction, the use of new channels, communication tools and the intensity of its flow, as well as the emergence of new genres in the discursive practice of diplomacy.

As a working definition of institutional discourse in the sphere of diplomacy, this study adopts the term diplomatic discourse, which is understood as speech that is implemented in institutional situations of communication in the subject area of diplomacy and international relations, aimed at ensuring the security of the state, cooperation and search for agreement with foreign countries, creating a positive perception of the state in the world.

Over time, digital diplomacy has been adopted by the diplomatic departments of the world's leading powers, which has caused increased attention to this phenomenon on the part of political scientists. The following definition of digital diplomacy is currently accepted in the field of political science: the use of the Internet and information and communication technologies (ICT) to solve diplomatic problems. Digital diplomacy makes use of new media, social networks, blogs and similar media platforms of the global network. In an effort to reach the widest possible audience, diplomats actually 'compete' in their microblogs. The number of official diplomatic accounts on social networks is gradually increasing.

Digital diplomacy is a complex multifunctional mechanism that, thanks to the specifics of the Internet space, integrates all the various ways of presenting information materials (printed texts, photographs, drawings, graphics, video recordings).

In the current situation in world politics, characterised by political, economic and local military conflicts, the strategy of defamation aimed at discrediting foreign policy opponents has come to play a key role not only in the media, but also in the information diplomatic practice of many states.

At the same time, it should be stressed that the Internet can be misused by individuals and can be weakened by governments and large organisations. The fact is that sites containing valuable information can also be used to deliberately spread misinformation (Figure 3.18).

A recent example of disinformation is a fake photo purportedly showing me at a rally organised by the Russian opposition that took place on 20 September, which was published by some Russian news channels. In reality, I was at home during that rally, and my image in the photo was taken from a photograph taken in February.

The danger of misinformation: a real photo of me (left) next to a photoshopped picture (right).

Figure 3.18: Examples of images given by John Tefft himself

To defend the thesis about the risks of unfair use of the Internet, the diplomat uses a strategy of experiential corroboration through the argument "to his own biography", a recent example of misinformation that affected Mr Tefft himself. The distinctive marker of the argument to biography in this example is the 'voice of the self'. Voices are social agents of communication, individuals involved in the construction of identity. In the text, the identities of discourse participants are usually expressed by pronouns, which allow for the tactic of distancing or convergence (solidarisation), emphasising the skills and abilities of the speaker that others lack, for example, for the construction of professional identity. In this example, the voice "I" acts as a marker of individuality, contributing to the construction of professional identity.

An important place in this example is occupied by the opposition, presented simultaneously at the textual and graphic levels. Two opposite facts (allegedly captured at the rally organised by the Russian opposition) (In reality, I was at home during this rally) are introduced, on the one hand, by the particle ostensibly, on the other hand, by the adverbial expression in reality, which strengthens the contrast. The images following the text confirm the diplomat's words and reinforce his thesis of disinformation.

As a consequence, this leads to a decrease in the addressee's criticality threshold and an increase in susceptibility to disinformation, which is extremely convenient for the realisation of information tasks of foreign policy.

The processes of globalisation in the modern world increasingly require the use of ICTs as a way of developing the country in the long term. The Strategy for Action for the Further Development of the Republic of Uzbekistan states the need to strengthen the openness of the activities of the organs of State power and administration and to introduce modern forms of providing information relating to the rights, freedoms and legitimate interests of natural and legal persons.

Recently, specific measures have been taken to improve the openness of public authorities and administration. As the analysis shows, the need for these measures is caused by the fact that new and diverse forms and methods of dialogue between the state and society are increasingly used.

Digital diplomacy is defined as a strategy for managing change through digital tools and virtual collaboration.

The online publication Digital Diplomacy drew attention to the formation of the first stages of Uzbekistan's digital diplomacy in 2016. In order to study the performance of the foreign ministries of 210 countries in digital diplomacy, the publication conducted a study, on the basis of which it compiled a global ranking. It is based on the digital information of the Foreign Ministries of 210 countries in the period from January 2015 to March 2016. Currently, 742 social media accounts, 208 official web pages and 43 mobile applications are used by various foreign policy departments and government agencies in a number of countries.

Most foreign ministries of different countries have their own Twitter and Facebook pages. The rating takes into account the activity of foreign ministries on the Internet, primarily in social networks. The top ten of the rating include the United Kingdom, France, the United States, Russia, the EU, the Vatican, India, Israel, Mexico and Switzerland. Uzbekistan ranked 124th in the rating.

The opening of pages and groups on Facebook and other social networks makes it possible to create a convenient format for prompt communication between government agencies and the Internet audience and to use this platform as a source of their own information intended for the media and the public at large.

Recently, domestic Internet publications have started to adjust their activities. The promptness and completeness of the information provided to them are becoming the main criteria for the preparation of information products. Particular attention is paid to identifying practical mechanisms for informing society about the activities of government agencies and providing citizens with broad access to information about decisions being made. The official websites of all ministries and departments, as well as regional khokimiyats, publish adopted normative, legal and other acts regulating, in particular, issues of relations with business entities, including procedures, terms and costs of providing State and other types of services.

Information is posted on the procedure for legal entities and individuals to submit applications, complaints and other appeals, as well as the possibility of feedback. Active work on the Internet is related to the openness of government agencies, which means that users of the Internet are offered free access to and discussion of information about the work of the agency.

In foreign practice, digital diplomacy is primarily used as a tool for realising foreign policy objectives through virtual space. In Uzbekistan, the Ministry of Foreign Affairs, through its website and Facebook page, regularly publishes relevant and objective foreign and domestic policy information in order to bring it to the people of Uzbekistan in a timely manner.

The implementation of digital diplomacy will make it possible to fully fulfil new tasks to ensure the country's national interests, increase the transparency and openness of foreign policy activities, and build up an online presence in the world through the widespread use of digital technologies.

Digital diplomacy allows all participants to communicate their position to a multi-million dollar foreign audience in the shortest possible time with minimal cost and instant public response.

One of the main tasks of digital diplomacy is to adapt to a rapidly changing environment by developing appropriate strategies to reach target groups, to deliver the right information to them (but without overloading them with excessive volumes), and, as in traditional diplomacy, to maximise the presence in society of the main actors - representatives of states, international or non-governmental organisations.

While there are many different social media outlets, Twitter continues to hold a special place in the world of diplomacy and politics. Of all social media, Twitter is the most quoted when it comes to immediate events, especially in times of multiple crises. In fact, Twitter has already achieved the title of the main online channel used to instantly inform and analyse information on the most important social and political events of the day. Due to its brevity, Twitter forces its users to be concise in conveying their thoughts in limited text and is probably the most frequently used source for analysing the online presence of various personalities (in the context of Big Data and the study of unstructured data).

To assess the breadth and depth of the social media presence, two quantitative indicators were introduced to reflect social media activity and its perception by the public.

Activity and perception was calculated for each account to determine its social media success rate.

The following types of data were collected for each Twitter account:

- the total number of status updates since the account was registered;
- number of followers;
- number of other pages to which the analysed account is subscribed;
- the number of public lists the account is listed on;
- the time the account has existed (in weeks).

In addition to the data described above, the following information was also collected:

- number of author tweets (excludes retweets from other pages);
- the total number of retweets of posts by the author of this page;
- the number of "like" marks of the page owner's author tweets;
- the number of replies to tweets posted on behalf of the page owner.

Activity and perceptual measures were developed and calculated based on the data collected.

In this case, the main indicators of activity were:

Productivity: the number of tweets posted since the account was created, including all retweets and replies, divided by the time the page has been live in weeks. Productivity *is the* most straightforward metric used in these measurements and reflects a user's weekly activity.

Originality: the ratio of own tweets (productivity minus retweets) relative to the total number of tweets in the account. This criterion reflects the amount of new content published by a particular account.

Communicative: the ratio of replies to other Twitter users' posts to the total number of tweets. How often does the account holder engage in dialogues?

Interest: the number of followers of an account divided by the time the account has existed in weeks. Essentially, a weekly measure of the Twitter audience's interest in the content published on the page.

The perception indicators were:

Total retweets: Total number of retweets divided by the number of your own tweets. How much of the original content published by this account is shared with other users through the page's followers?

Popularity: the number of "likes" on a page's tweets divided by the number of its own tweets.

Followers Growth: Total number of followers on Twitter divided by the time the account has existed in weeks. Reflects the weekly growth rate of the audience.

Publicity: the number of public lists the account is listed on, divided by the time the account has existed in weeks. Another type of audience growth measurement, this time based on the public lists that include this page.

If successful social media outreach were determined solely by perception indicators, then many (potentially unaccounted for) factors would become very important. There are certainly players in the digital arena who gain a certain amount of popularity simply because they are very influential outside of it, or because their ideas or statements are of interest to a wide range of people. Utilising the popularity achieved offline is also a possible and effective strategy.

In a broader sense, we can speak of the transformation of diplomacy in the digital age - similar to the changes that other spheres of public life are undergoing. Such an interpretation covers not only public relations, but also many different issues, from new requirements for the competences needed by a diplomat and ensuring a reliable and secure diplomatic network infrastructure to the use of information and communication technologies for solving international problems and negotiating the rules of interaction between states in cyberspace.

It is no coincidence that communication between leaders and foreign policy officials via social media has attracted a lot of attention. The ability to address Internet users directly and to follow live discussions of interest to diplomats is increasingly moving diplomacy away from the traditional model, when it was primarily a communication function between heads of state.

China promotes digital diplomacy. Chinese authorities recognise the dominance of foreign media in China and that much of the information is not true. In political circles, this is referred to as the downside of soft power. Through the Internet, a significant contribution to the spread of the Chinese position is made by the Chinese population. On the Internet, China has its own "army" created to dominate online conversations and shape public opinion at home and abroad. It employs about 300,000 people who, to promote the government line, post relevant information on forums, websites, and blogs. The government supports such "cyber-soldiers", who in turn are active on foreign forums, opposing any negative information about China. This strategy is also used to promote the "Chinese dream" as a new ideological construct

Humanity has undergone six major information and communication transitions in the course of its development:

- the emergence of language and intelligible human speech;
- the invention of writing and printing;
- the emergence of mass communication media;
- dissemination of computing and information technology;
- development of global information networks;
- formation of the information society.

ICTs, penetrating virtually all strata of civilisation, along with undoubted positives, have sharply exacerbated geopolitical turbulence.

"The nature of the international environment is increasingly influenced by the growing confrontation in the global information space due to the desire of some countries to use ICTs to achieve their geopolitical goals, including by manipulating public consciousness and falsifying history."

Schematically, the development of technological stages is presented in (Fig. 3.19).

NATO's 20 Centres of Excellence play an important role in hybrid operations. NATO's Joint Centre of Excellence for Cyber Defence was established in Tallinn in 2008. Its main task is to provide advice, training and research in the field of cyber security.

At the same time, 95 rules have been developed, including:

- A state can respond to an attack either by bringing the aggressor to justice or by "proportional countermeasures";

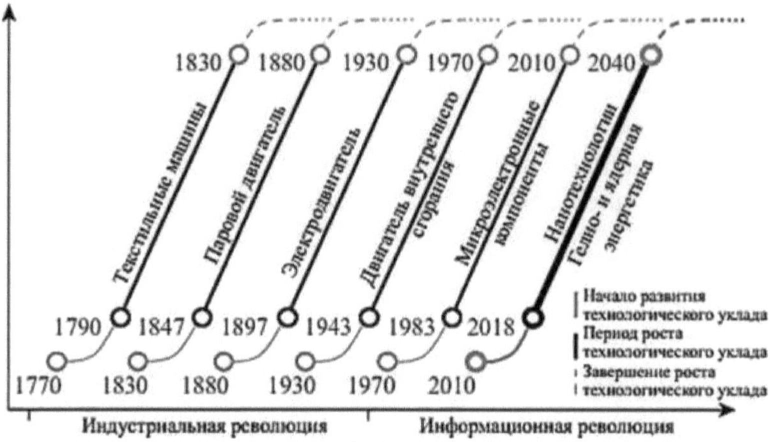

Fig.3.19. Scheme of evolution of technological modes.

- Since an attack is an "armed assault", self-defence, including the use of traditional weapons, is lawful;
- cyber attacks should be equated with chemical, biological and radiological weapons in terms of their impact;
- cyber espionage, cyber theft and attacks on websites (except for damage on a national scale) cannot be recognised as an armed attack;
- the aggressor state must be held accountable, even if it attacks with the help of proxies from other countries.

Thus, the document essentially legitimised conflicts in cyberspace as forms of behaviour by states and mediators acting on their behalf.

It set the task of discrediting the political and military leadership, spreading panic and defeatism among the population.

The structure of information wars is presented in Figure 3.20.

In the field of international information security (IIS), ICT is used for the following purposes:

а) as an information weapon for politico-military purposes contrary to international law, to carry out hostile actions and acts of aggression aimed at discrediting sovereignty, violating the territorial integrity of States and posing a threat to international peace, security and strategic stability;

б) for terrorist purposes, including for destructive impact on elements of critical information infrastructure, as well as for terrorist propaganda and attracting new supporters to terrorist activities;

в) to interfere in the internal affairs of sovereign States, disturb public order, incite inter-ethnic, inter-racial and inter-confessional hatred, propagate racist and xenophobic ideas or theories that generate hatred and discrimination and incite violence;

Fig.3.20. Structure of information wars.

г) to commit offences, including those related to unlawful access to computer information and the creation, use and distribution of malicious computer programmes.

Network-centric warfare (NCW) uses ultramodern information and networking technologies to integrate geographically dispersed command, control, intelligence, surveillance, and target designation assets, as well as troop groupings and precision weapons into a highly adaptive, global system with extensive use of electronic warfare (Figure 3.21).

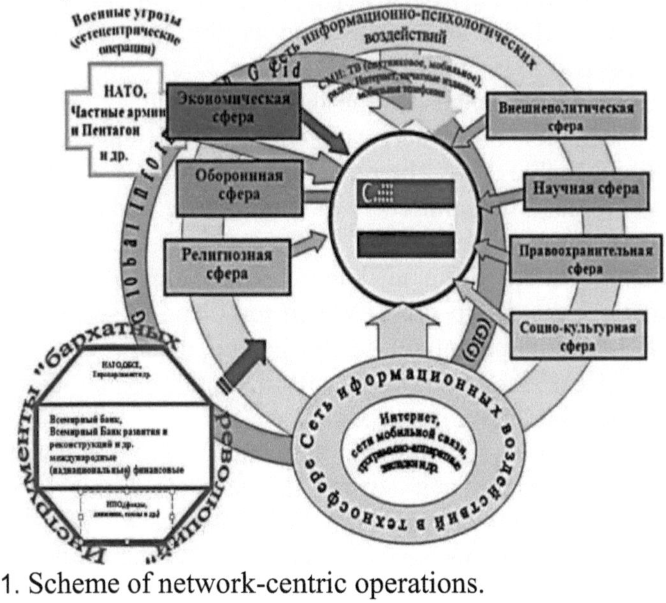

Fig.3.21. Scheme of network-centric operations.

If we try to analyse all 198 methods, scrupulously structured and described by him, it is not difficult to see in them the arsenal of the following three stages of all 24 "colour revolutions" that took place in the world between 1989 and 2015.

1. Protest actions, rallies, marches, pickets. Convincing people in the illegitimacy of the authorities and the formation of an anti-government movement.
2. Discrediting the security forces, strikes, public disobedience, riots and sabotage.
3. The violent overthrow of the government.

Without knowledge of the methods outlined, it is impossible to understand the algorithm of "colour revolutions", and thus to apply adequate countermeasures and conduct effective preventive network diplomacy.

The rapidly changing face of international relations requires diplomacy to be proactive and proactive, otherwise time favourable for influencing the international environment may be lost.

§3.5 Methods and technologies to protect against leakage of confidential information

Since ancient times, any human activity has been based on the receipt and possession of information, i.e. on information support. Information is one of the most important means of solving problems and tasks both at the state level and at the level of commercial organisations and individuals.

The topics of developments on the industrial espionage market cover almost all aspects of society, of course, focusing on the most financially profitable ones. The range of services offered is wide: from primitive radio transmitters to modern apparatus-industrial reconnaissance complexes.

All this is associated with a sufficient risk of value of different kinds of information, the disclosure of which may lead to serious losses in various fields (administrative, scientific and technical, commercial, etc.). Therefore, the issues of information protection (IP) are becoming more and more important.

Content analysis tools for outgoing data packets provide the ability to process network traffic sent outside the controlled area in order to detect possible leakage of confidential information. As a rule, they are used to analyse outgoing mail and web traffic sent to the Internet. Examples of content analysis tools of this type are the systems "Do-

Zor-Jet" (www.jetinfo.ru), "Mail Sweeper" (www.www.infosec.ru.ru) and InfoWatch Web Monitor (www.www.infowatch.com.com).
Such protection means are installed in the gap of the communication channel between the Internet and the AS of the enterprise, so that all outgoing data packets pass through them (Fig. 3.22).

Fig.3.22. Scheme of installation of content analysis tools in the AS

In the process of analysing outgoing messages, the latter are divided into service fields that are processed according to the criteria set by the security administrator. For example, content analysis tools allow blocking data packets that contain such keywords as "secret", "confidential" and others. These tools also provide the ability to filter messages that are sent to external addresses that are not part of the corporate electronic document management system.
The advantage of this type of protection system is the ability to monitor and impose restrictions on both incoming and outgoing traffic. However, these systems do not guarantee 100 per cent detection of messages containing confidential information. In particular, if an intruder encrypts a message before sending it or disguises it as a graphic or music file using steganography methods, content analysis tools will be practically powerless in this case.
Within the threat model, the key element is the concept of an "insider". An insider is an employee of a company who is an intruder and who may have legal access to confidential information. As a result of an insider's actions, confidential information may fall into the wrong hands. It is important to note, however, that an insider's actions can be either intentional or negligent. For example, many incidents involving the leakage of confidential information are due to employee negligence. For example, an employee may lose a laptop with work files or mistakenly send an email with trade secrets to someone else.
To date, we can distinguish the following main channels of confidential information leakage, which can be used by an insider:
- unauthorised copying of confidential information to external media

and taking it outside the controlled territory of the enterprise. Examples of such media are floppy discs, CD-ROM compact discs, Flash discs, and others;

- printing confidential information and taking the printed documents outside the controlled area. It should be noted that in this case both local printers, which are directly connected to the attacker's computer, and remote printers, with which interaction is carried out via the network, can be used;
- Theft of media containing confidential information - hard discs, magnetic tapes, CD-ROMs, etc;
- unauthorised transmission of confidential information over the network to external Internet servers located outside the controlled territory of the enterprise.

Examples of leakage channels that can be used by attackers to transfer sensitive data outside the enterprise:

- SMTP e-mail transmission protocol. Today almost any company uses e-mail service to exchange information with clients, partners and employees. This type of communication has a lot of advantages, such as cheapness, ease of use, availability, and others. At the same time, a potential intruder can use e-mail as a tool to steal information. To do this, he or she only needs to send an email with a confidential document attached to an external email address and then access the data from home;
- HTTP hypertext transfer protocol. The HTTP protocol is the basic protocol for interacting with Internet resources, but it can be used by a potential attacker to publish confidential information on forums, blogs, LiveJoumalu magazines, and other sites and then make it available to unauthorised persons;
- FTP file transfer protocol. This protocol can also be used to copy confidential data to external file servers located on the Internet;
- P2P peer-to-peer network protocols. Peer-to-peer networks such as BitzTorennt, eMulen and others allow users to share file resources among themselves. However, if there are no controls over such sharing, a potential intruder can use them to transfer confidential information over the Internet;
- protocols for exchanging speech and text information via the Internet. The most common protocol of this type is Skype;
- protocols of instant messaging systems ICQ, AOL, WindoWsMessengem et al. This type of protocols can also be used for

unauthorised transfer of files with confidential data between subscribers.

To effectively protect against internal security threats, it is necessary to apply a comprehensive approach that provides for the application of organisational, regulatory, methodological and technical measures to protect information resources. Thus, the enterprise should develop and implement organisational and administrative documents defining the list of confidential information resources, possible threats associated with them, as well as a list of measures to be implemented to counteract these threats. Such documents are the "Information Security Concept" and "Information Security Policy", as well as job descriptions of the company's employees and others. In addition to organisational protection means, technical solutions designed to block the above-mentioned channels of confidential information leakage should be applied. Technical means of protection of the DLP class can be divided into three classes:

- protection means at the level of user workstations designed for local control over information flows within the user's workstation;
- gateway-level security features to ensure control of information flows at the perimeter of the organisation's LAN;
- complex defences that combine the capabilities of the first two classes.

Confidential information leakage protection systems of this type are specialised software complexes designed to detect unauthorised user actions related to an attempt to transfer confidential information outside the controlled territory of the enterprise. Systems of this type consist of the following components:

- agents installed on user workstations that collect information about events registered on these stations;
- management server designed for centralised management of the system agents;
- a database providing storage of the results of the defence system operation;
- Security Administrator Management Console.

Based on settings defined by the security administrator, agents allow you to control user access to sensitive information, as well as impose restrictions on the actions a user can perform with that information.

The advantage of using protection systems of this type is the possibility of creating a virtual isolated environment for processing

confidential information without physically allocating a separate automated system for working with restricted data. However, the use of protection systems entails the installation of additional software on each workstation, which can potentially lead to increased complexity of administration, as well as to possible conflicts in the operation of system programmes.
Confidential information leakage protection systems of this type are specialised software complexes designed to detect unauthorised user actions related to an attempt to transfer confidential information outside the controlled territory of the enterprise. Systems of this type consist of the following components:

- agents installed on user workstations that collect information about events registered on these stations;
- management server designed for centralised management of the system agents;
- a database providing storage of the results of the defence system operation;
- Security Administrator Management Console.

Based on settings defined by the security administrator, agents allow you to control user access to sensitive information, as well as impose restrictions on the actions a user can perform with that information.
The advantage of using protection systems of this type is the possibility of creating a virtual isolated environment for processing confidential information without physically allocating a separate automated system for working with restricted data. However, the use of protection systems entails the installation of additional software on each workstation, which can potentially lead to increased complexity of administration, as well as to possible conflicts in the operation of system programmes.
Information leakage protection systems at the gateway level provide the ability to process network traffic sent outside the controlled area in order to detect possible leakage of confidential information. They are usually used to analyse outgoing mail and web traffic sent to the Internet.
These protections are installed in the break in the communication channel between the Internet and the enterprise LAN, so that all outgoing data packets pass through them.
Currently, there are two main technologies for detecting attempts to steal confidential information. The first of them is based on searching

the analysed data stream for keywords set by the security administrator. For example, it is possible to block messages that contain such keywords as "secret", "confidential" and others.
The second technology makes it possible to identify potential leaks on the basis of so-called "digital fingerprints" that are lifted from confidential information. These "digital fingerprints" are a specially calculated checksum and allow identifying a confidential document even if it has been deliberately altered by an intruder.
However, none of these technologies can guarantee 100 per cent detection of messages containing sensitive information. For example, if an intruder encrypts a message before sending it or disguises it as a graphic or music file using steganography techniques, content analysis tools will be virtually powerless.
Currently, one of the most pressing problems in the field of information security is the problem of protection against confidential information leakage. To effectively protect against such threats, it is necessary to apply a comprehensive approach that provides for the application of both organisational and technical measures to protect information resources.

CONCLUSIONS TO CHAPTER III

In this chapter:

- The formation of interstate regimes of the integrated information security system is considered;
- information security threats are categorised by orientation;
- a model of an information security intruder is given;
- priority factors of the conceptual model of state information security were selected;
- measured the amount of information using Entropy and Thesarus approaches;
- components are summarised in the form of a conceptual model of information security;
- the concepts of external sources of threats are given;
- methods of constructing a conceptual model of state information security are given;
- highlighted a number of essential properties of information from the point of view of protection;
- geometrical models of the information protection system are considered;
- The process of modelling of information security threats in the

ACS KVO is provided;

- levels of logical access are highlighted;
- algorithms for analysis and evaluation are given;
- algorithms for regulating the strategy of interstate relations on the basis of digital diplomacy are given;
- The structure of information warfare and the scheme of network-centric operations are presented;
- methods and technologies of protection against leakage of confidential information are given.

CHAPTER IV

METHODS TO IMPROVE THE INFORMATION ASSURANCE SYSTEM STATE SECURITY

The final fourth chapter "Methods of improving the system of ensuring information security of the state" outlines methods of creating virtual communicative information spaces of interstate relations, methods and means of constructing the image of informants and their organisational structures, and also substantiates digital diplomacy as a means of operational introduction into mass consciousness. At the same time, systematic approaches to improving interstate relations on the platforms of professional social networks are attached.

§4.1 Methods of creating virtual communicative information spaces of interstate relations

The concept of "information and communication space" is an integral factor in the development of the theory of information society and globalisation processes observed by every member of society.

In order for the information and communication space that automatically arises around any kind of activity to work not against but for the good, to be constructive, it is important to create a controlled model in which contacts between different subjects of information and communication are carried out with maximum efficiency. And, in addition, the structure of subject-subject and subject-object relations functions.

If we understand information analytics and its substrate (information) as the production of new knowledge based on the processing of available information in order to optimise decision-making, then we can safely state that in the conditions of modern development of communication channels, powerful information flows are concentrated and processed in all nodes of information infrastructure (in all spheres of activity) in order to make socially significant managerial decisions.

The informational and auxiliary nature of information analytics, which makes it similar to other types of information-infrastructural, informational and auxiliary services, traditionally ordering the information space, optimising and directing the movement of information flows, ensuring the preservation of accumulated information resources, etc., allows to perform the essential, basic function of information transformation: information coagulation, consolidation of large information arrays in the form of databases and databanks, and their creation.

Actively operating with information products and services, information analytics primarily fulfils the task of qualitative and substantive transformation of information, functionally overlapping in this respect with scientific (production of new knowledge) and managerial (development of decision options, scenarios) activities.

Information analytics, based on hermeneutic methods, i.e. in a broad sense - on the interpretation of texts, if the latter are interpreted universally - informationally as documents, texts, data, messages about events, etc., as well as to those sections of science, types of scientific tasks, when the conclusion knowledge is obtained not by experimental means, but on the basis of analysis and interpretation of existing theories, descriptions of facts, by means of information modelling of reality, is called to reveal objective regularities and trends, determines the movement of the information modeling of reality.

The spatial organisation of information along with the regularities of the spatial construction of information systems is the object of study of informology - a general scientific, theoretical direction, in the modern view representing such definitions-functions as "space is an organised environment" and "information is a state of space".

This approach presupposes, at least, informological competence, which determines the development of the modelled space of receiving and disseminating information, adequate to the conditions of information and communication reality.

The most important component of informational competence, in its turn, is information and communication competence, which can be considered as "a complex ability to independently search, select the necessary information, analyse, organise, present, transmit it; model and design objects and processes, implement projects, including in the sphere of individual and group human activity".

At the same time, informological competence is a deeper concept, reflects the statement of the multivalent concept of information in the status of a category along with matter, energy, space and time and is manifested in the formation of an individual information picture of the world - an integrative image of information and communication reality as a means of intellectual mastering of the world.

Information and communication technologies and, in particular, the global Internet, becoming an integral attribute of interaction both at the informal (household) and official levels, make us rethink approaches to modelling both informational and communicative space, taking into account the emergence and sustainable functioning of virtual space.

Modern management concepts, including those in the information and communication sphere, are inextricably linked to the increasing role of social communication as such and, in particular, mass communication media in society. Communication processes, which unite society at all levels, permeate the social environment, distribute and broadcast significant information, have a significant impact on the life of society. The growing informatisation of social life leads to an increased impact of interpretative schemes and paradigms on the feelings and moods of large masses of people, brings together previously closed to each other cultural worlds, not excluding, but, on the contrary, actively and purposefully applying methods of manipulating mass consciousness.

Therefore, one cannot but agree with the idea that "in the technotronic society, information power is increasingly invading all spheres of social relations".

The role of communication in the development of globalisation processes has recently attracted increasing attention. Hence the relevance of addressing the socio-philosophical study of the phenomenon of communication. It is determined by the urgent need for theoretical reflection on the changes occurring in the sphere of communication and the social changes accompanying them; in comprehension of the opening opportunities of social regulation associated with the new phase of communication development and the associated dangers of limiting the freedom of individual consciousness. All these factors cannot but affect the principles of modelling the information and communication space, within the framework of which the interaction of individuals, groups and communities is regulated in modern society, which is subject to globalisation deformations.

The speaker's self-awareness and self-image, the idea of what impression he himself and his message should make on others, contributes to the communicative space.

Interaction of socionic types takes place in the communicative space.

This space is heterogeneous: its density in different places is not the same, therefore information exchange of the same types in different places will have different intensity.
Deep communication means dense information exchange, when practically all information resources available to a sociotype are involved in communication.
There is a close intertwining of the "power lines" of the information fields, which indicates a high trustworthiness of the contact.
Four basic elements can be identified in the exchange of information in the communication process:
1) Sender, a person who generates ideas or gathers information and transmits it;
2) message, the actual information encoded with symbols;
3) a channel, a means of transmitting information;
4) Recipient.
When exchanging information, the sender and receiver go through several interrelated stages. Their task is to compose the message and use the channel to transmit it in such a way that both parties understand and share the original idea. This is difficult, for each stage is at the same time a point at which meaning can be distorted or completely lost. The interrelated stages are as follows:
1) the genesis of an idea;
2) encoding and channel selection;
3) handover;
4) decoding.
This is the simplest model of the information exchange process.
The process of information and communication interaction can be schematically represented as a conceptual model reflecting the cycle of two-way communication:

Fig.4.1. Scheme of the process of information and communication interaction.
Thus, the implementation of communication is a cohesive process necessary for any important managerial action.

In order for the recipient to have an identical representation of the original object it is necessary to apply both extensional and intensional approaches, the technology of interpretation of the received message, as well as fixed characteristics of information (semantic, semiotic, axiological), to form a thesaurus. Although the application of all these approaches does not guarantee the success of the system construction.

The widespread introduction and widespread use of information and communication technologies is seen as a decisive step from industrial to post-industrial (information) society.

However, such a transition, carried out in the light of technological development, cannot pass rapidly without a trace for society. This was mentioned by the "prophet of electronic communication" M. McLuhan, who presented a three-stage model of world history, where the third epoch is the epoch of the information individual in the conditions of the victory of electronic (audiovisual) communication, which increases the intellectual abilities and creative character of the individual.

M. McLuhan compared new means and technologies to a colossal collective surgery performed on the social body with complete disregard for antiseptics. The whole system is affected when a new technology operates on society. The impact of radio is visual, the impact of photography is auditory. Each new pressure causes shifts in the proportions of all the senses. "What we seek today is a means of controlling these shifts in the sensory proportions of the mental and social worldview, or a means of avoiding these shifts altogether."

In this regard, it becomes important to identify the forms and technologies of administrative management in the conditions of virtualisation of society, based on the analysis of world and domestic experience.

In its initial stage, electronic technology (space communication, portable video recording) has fulfilled the role of social therapy. It created a new stage of social communication in which the distortions and disparities caused by geography and economics were levelled, fostering greater understanding between different segments of society and peoples.

At present, for example, the Internet is both a medium for worldwide broadcasting and a tool for information dissemination. And, most importantly, a medium for people to collaborate and communicate.

It is known that mass communication is characterised by a special requirement for compliance with the norms of communication accepted in society compared to interpersonal communication. It is dictated by the fact that the transmitted messages should be as clear and understandable as possible for the widest audience, for each participant of communication. In addition, the establishment of a certain set of normative requirements should contribute to the exclusion of extremist appeals, unnecessary politicisation, preaching violence, religious and ethnic enmity and other immoral actions from the information process. At present, these normative requirements are united into codes of Internet ethics or codes of behaviour on the Internet.

The process of informatisation, formation of information society, leading to the effect of globalisation and permeability of spatial, cultural, political, linguistic, etc. barriers, inclusion of regions, states, certain social groups into a single political, economic, legal, information space, multiplies the degree of interdependence of all subjects of the world community.

The variety of information impulses (messages) about events, opinions, containing controlling influences, broadcast through the channels of information infrastructure and having a determinant influence on social processes, has become unimaginably large these days. Therefore, the cumulative effect formed as a result of these diverse, contradictory, multi-scale influences forms such an incomprehensibly complex system of determinism of social development that the latter objectively appears before modern subjects of social management as an irrational, indeterministic phenomenology.

The information society, having acquired unprecedented freedom, unity in diversity, and dynamism of development, has acquired a new degree of vulnerability to destructive factors and various social deviations. The natural consequence of all these trends is inadequate management decisions, unforeseen consequences of decisions, voluntarism and subjectivism of leaders of various ranks, confrontations, attempts to lobby, interference in objective processes of certain forces, manipulation of public opinion, etc..

From a geopolitical point of view, information space is understood as a certain virtual territory that belongs to the state, is a specific state resource and must be protected from possible aggressors.

Various communicative resources (chat rooms, forums, social

networks) attract users by their democracy, interactivity, and globality. Tools of search, communication, transfer of audio, visual, textual content allow visitors to satisfy any actual needs. Getting acquainted with an interesting person, consulting a specialist, exchanging information with close friends and relatives are now available with minimal expenditure of resources. Hours-long trips to potential interlocutors and expensive telephone conversations are losing their relevance, giving way to cheap, indirect and instant contact with network actors in virtual reality.

However, these features not only facilitate the communication process and help to form networks and communities of like-minded people, but also cause tangible damage to unwary users. The freedom of self-expression and self-presentation, the openness and accessibility of electronic platforms, and the very nature of virtual interactions initiate serious information threats to user security.

One of the most common and serious dangers is the communicative risks of the network, namely aggression and provocation on the part of virtual interlocutors. Researcher E.N. Basovskaya singles out speech aggression as a special kind of dominant speech behaviour. Such verbal aggression can be expressed in a familiar attitude to the interlocutor, insults, boorishness, wishing harm, use of rude words, sarcasm, and others.

Linguist T.I.Steksova sees the most obvious example of speech aggression in virtual dialogues of open forums and news sites. According to the scientist, the aggressive reaction of communicators is not related to the desire to manipulate and humiliate interlocutors, but is an indicator of the general emotional background, attitude to the world and others. Despite the fact that the user does not always aim to offend other participants, but only expresses his own emotions and defends a certain point of view, such speech activity poses a threat to both his interlocutors and passive readers.

Negative feedback and depressing emotional background, according to the researcher, transform the user's world picture, provoke negative emotional reactions and destructive communicative strategies. At the same time, the victim of aggressive behaviour often represents a deeply wounded person and a potential tyrant. Such famous psychologists as A. Freud, N. Beyer, S. Ferenczi highlight "identification with the aggressor" as one of the main protective mechanisms of the psyche, which can be the cause of delinquent behaviour and other negative changes.

Along with such private manifestations of aggressive behaviour on the Web as insults, remarks, irony and criticism, more serious and dangerous forms of information and communication threats are actively developing. Among them, such phenomena as trolling and cyberbullying are the most clearly identified. According to the researcher M.M. Akulich, trolling is the placement of provocative, offensive information on electronic resources in order to provoke a negative reaction, aggression and conflict among communication participants. Trolling can be initiated either by an individual or by entire organisations. The objectives of trolling range from commercial, political, economic to psychological and socio-cultural. However, regardless of the personal characteristics and motivation of the provocateur, his activities are always aimed at the emotional destabilisation of the individual through manipulation and aggressive behaviour.

Unlike trolling, cyberbullying is not limited to mild forms of verbal aggression, but is a complex of repeated, constantly ongoing attacks on the interlocutor with the purpose of virtual terror. In their article "Cyberbullying - bullying in modern space", scientists A.A. Bochaver and K.D. Khromov define cyberbullying as a new form of bullying using the latest modern technologies for aggressive persecution of the user in virtual space. In their opinion, cyberbullying can be both direct and indirect. In a situation of direct interaction, the aggressor sends insulting messages, threats, rudeness and other negative information to the victim. As for indirect bullying, in this case, as a rule, the victim's account is hacked or a fake copy of it is created, followed by sending compromising materials, humiliation, fake photos, publishing obscene messages, attacks on the user's virtual friends.

Cyberbullying and trolling are the most dangerous information and communication threats that can lead to emotional destabilisation of the communicant, a drop in self-esteem, negative personal changes, feelings of fear and anxiety, transformation of communication strategies, life attitudes, disorientation, and in extreme cases to the deterioration of emotional, mental, physical health of the person, development of depressive disorders and suicide.

However, not only explicitly expressed aggressive and destructive effects of online actors can threaten the security of Web users. Such phenomena as social engineering, recruitment of users by terrorists, representatives of various sects, attacks by mentally unhealthy people, maniacs and fraudsters are widespread in the information and communication space of the Web. Their difference from the above mentioned virtual dangers is the complexity of identification of the negative nature of the impact, misunderstanding of the goals and motives of the communicator and the need for information and psychological protection.

One example of stealthy user impact is social engineering.

The methods of social engineering are the extraction of confidential information through deception, intimidation, and bribery. In the process of hacking into technical devices and stealing necessary information, social engineers primarily focus on the vulnerabilities of a person.

In addition to social engineering methods, the activities of representatives of various religious organisations, including extremist ones, pose a great danger. As T.V. Zhavoronkova writes in her publication, extremists are now actively using electronic resources to promote their goals and ideas, find like-minded people and recruit supporters. According to the data presented by the authors, extremists publish religious articles, calls for activity, video and photo content on forums and social networks, which is actively disseminated by users and contributes to the formation of false ideas and beliefs.

At the same time, terrorists use communication platforms to analyse users' personalities, find sympathisers and reach out to the most

by suitable personalities. The victims of extremist propaganda are often not only their ideological associates, but also users in a difficult life situation, who have lost the meaning of further existence and actively demonstrate indifference to their expected fate. In this case, the recruitment of supporters begins with establishing close contact with the user, frank dialogue on a variety of topics and gradually switches to manipulative messages and hidden propaganda of radical attitudes. It should be noted that it is not always easy to identify a terrorist, as social networking tools make it possible to hide information about the real person, create an attractive image and inspire confidence in other visitors.

The consequence of such information attacks by extremists can be psychological disorders, the formation of delinquent behaviour, emotional devastation, addiction, depression, fear for one's own life, transformation of social and moral guidelines, moral degradation and

much more.
All of the above is true not only for negative influences on the user of extremists, but also for manipulative actions of representatives of any unofficial religious community (sect). Sect members also search for like-minded people using the latest technologies and promote their ideas to interested parties on the pages of social networks or thematic resources. In this regard, the information threat is posed not only by radical Muslim organisations, but also by the participants of any unrecognised religious community actively using manipulative techniques, deception, propaganda appeals and influence on the human psyche.
The construction of the virtual information space model and its functioning is ensured by the creation and implementation of an integrated management automation system based on the most modern hardware and software.
In the conditions of intensive use of global information infrastructure (Internet space) as a communication environment of economic and social interaction, most of the acts of interaction between subjects are transferred to virtual space. Interaction in virtual space leads to a reduction in transaction costs and changes in the structure of integration formations, i.e. the network form of interaction prevails (there is no vertical control and the role of territorial restrictions is reduced). This determines the relevance of the study of subject interactions in terms of group interrelationships that form a network, which covers all economic agents in it and thus forms their economic space.
Internet technologies, creating virtual spaces and communities, offer the state, its partners and opponents new ways and methods of interaction.
At the same time, power itself, its political structures and institutions are undergoing significant transformations. National states are experiencing the need for new technologies of power and governance. The administration of state power through online and "e-government" technologies is gradually becoming a feature of our time. State structures begin to master technologies of PR*-communication, political advertising and other modern methods of communication with civil society, maintaining contacts with partners and opponents. At the same time, the traditional carriers of political influence in industrial society - parties - are giving way to the media and other

institutions that form the information space of power. The use of new information technologies leads to a qualitative transformation of society based on the principles of civil and information society. All these changes lead to the formation of a new form of power organisation in modern societies - mediacracy, which forms a specific political relationship between society and the ruling class, creating new opportunities for the use of state power.

Along with this genetic meaning, information also acts as a special political resource: actors who possess it gain advantages in gaining and redistributing power. The availability or absence of proper information determines the possibilities of an actor to gain or lose power, to achieve influence, to realise his interests in the political sphere. Thus, obtaining the necessary information becomes a specific goal of any actors acting in politics and interested in influencing power. Therefore, the process of acquiring information acts as a mechanism that ensures purposeful actions of political actors and allows them to adjust their behaviour. But if information does not find its way into the practical actions of people and institutions, it begins to undermine the foundations of their political statuses and undermine the traditions of power distribution operating in society. Therefore, the underdevelopment of information and communication exchanges in a particular political system inevitably weakens the power of the state, leads to a decrease in the adaptation of its institutions to social changes, and ultimately contributes to the destabilisation of power.

The presence of the main information flow in the international ICS can be characterised both positively and negatively. On the one hand, guided by market principles, it inevitably contributes to the spread of values of freedom and democracy, opposing and destroying rigid traditions of autarky, nationalism and parochialism. The information disseminated here ultimately leads to the internationalisation of lifestyles, shapes a multiculturalist model of human activity, and promotes world integration. These globalised infomediaries make it possible to maintain control over the rational distribution of the world's resources. On the other hand, the largely monopolistic position of Western transnational corporations (TNCs) in the world market creates opportunities for imposing an alien information environment on other countries and regions that does not take into account the information needs of a significant part of the population. The current situation is also characterised by the narrowing of citizens' access to quality information, which is being replaced by popular entertainment stories. Ultimately, such practices distort the information needs of various groups of the population (and even entire nations), impede the development of cultural traditions of these nations, and provoke the decline of national ethical norms and standards.

The most significant functions of public opinion include: representation of the current policy in the eyes of the public; providing feedback in the system of public administration, which implies correction of the course pursued by the regime; increasing the degree of legitimacy of the ruling regime; socialisation of citizens who are included in the sphere of political relations.

§4.2 . Formation of communicative information strategies for regulating interstate relations

Communicative strategy is a relatively new term in management theory. In fact, the term strategy is borrowed from the military sphere and, in essence, represents the choice not of a single path to victory (achievement of the goal), but the creation of such conditions that all paths lead to it. In its most general form, strategy acts as a sequence of steps (iterations), each link of which is characterised by the following. First, the presence of a strategic problem (situation), its analysis and setting a certain goal in relation to it. Secondly, construction (sequential construction of a design) as a way and design as a means of transforming the situation.

As the third most common feature of strategy, it is easy to notice the presence or determination "on the fly" of a priori provisions in accordance with which the situation is changed. In short, the various postulates, axioms, norms, rules and principles within the "a priori provisions" are a priori functionally (in terms of their function in the structure of the strategy); they are taken as non-situational, non-problematisable knowledge and attitudes within a given strategy.

Situation analysis in strategic thinking is, first of all, an analysis of possibilities. A communication strategy is needed not for "mass" situations, where stereotypes and algorithms can be used, but for problematic global situations. When drafting and implementing a communication strategy, it is necessary to constantly reflect on the values of the organisation, to imagine the goal (target situation and target audience) and the distance that separates the current situation from the final, target situation, and to solve the problem of reconciling values, goals and means time after time.

Public diplomacy is concerned with the practical application of communication and other social science research to influence the minds of foreign audiences so that the foreign policy of any other state using similar techniques is admired, or at least perceived without resentment. The goals of public diplomacy are clear: "one must try to capture the mindset of significant groups" and "the nation must be seen as a system of communication.

Today, the following forms of cultural cooperation and partnership are actively used in international relations, confirming the importance of cultural diplomacy: forums, festivals, tours, exhibitions, fairs, national language and culture days, competitions, contests, congresses, conferences, research and educational exchange programmes, the practice of scholarships and grants, and the activities of foundations. All these forms of international cultural exchange began to emerge a long time ago, but only in the conditions of integration and internationalisation have they received the fullest and most consistent development. In essence, the "cultural product" is the quintessence of individual forms of cultural cooperation, directed from the subjects-sources of communication to the subjects-recipients through strategic communication management.

It is also possible to designate linear (from the linear model of communication) and interactive (from the feedback model) approaches to the study of communicative strategies in the field of cultural diplomacy. In the framework of the linear approach there is such a communicative strategy as kulturträgerism (kulturträger 'from German Kulturträger imperialist-colonialist-colonialist'). Kulturträger 'from German Kulturträger imperialist-coloniser who enslaves backward peoples under the guise of imposing culture') and missionaryism. These strategies are practically not used in the modern world. Their peculiarity is in the violent spread of cultural (religious) values of one country on the territory of another. Within the framework of the interactive approach we can talk about the strategy of meeting the socially significant needs of the subjects/objects of communication in knowledge, understanding and acceptance of cultural values of another country, another nation, about the strategy of conscious consumption of foreign 'cultural products'.

As applied to the sphere of politics, this meant that the actor who established communication and was able to maintain it on the basis of his ideas, opinions, myths, symbols, slogans, positions, gets the opportunity to regulate the course of conflicts and manage them, thus strengthening his status and increasing the legitimacy of government. In the context of the social approach to communication, science has developed many of its theoretical models. The most common among them can be considered linear and non-linear.

The linear one implies the interaction of the communicator (the sender of initial information), the communicant (the interpreter of initial information) and the recipient (the receiver of information). Within the framework of this model, various additional components can be identified: information sources, interference factors, information filters, feedbacks, etc. The main thing is that such a simplified model gives an opportunity to better understand the sequence of events in information exchanges, the main parameters of communication.

Along with it, a non-linear model is also used (T. Newcomb). It represents a triangle, the vertices of which are the communicator, the communicant and the situation. In this case, the communicator and the communicant simultaneously act as both sources and receivers of messages. In this case

interaction between them can occur both with and without taking into account the situation. Such a model demonstrates a wider range of variants of interaction of the main parameters, especially the dependence on external factors.

§4.3 . Methods and tools for constructing the image of informants and their organisational structures

Today, the sources of information are so numerous and the information itself so diverse that some of it may not be completely reliable. Therefore, data must be checked and rechecked with the help of various sources, for which purpose special units are created in large organisations. They are engaged in planning the need for information, its collection, processing, analysis, evaluation, compilation, recommendations for management, as well as the creation of a strategic data base.

The mass media play a special role in forming an opinion about the situation in the municipality and the image of local authorities. At present, there are trends in the use of a whole complex of information manipulative technologies, the purpose of which is to introduce attitudes and stereotypes into the mass consciousness, to encourage the masses to make the necessary decisions and actions. One of the peculiarities of modern manipulation techniques is primarily carried out through print media and television, which create "images" and have an evaluative character. The use of these technologies is aimed at creating a certain emotional mood and psychological attitudes in the audience.

An indicator of the interest and participation of the population in political life is the determination of how closely citizens follow the general course of political events in the country as a whole. The main channel for obtaining information about the work of the authorities today is the media.

Today, the widespread use of image manipulative technologies, the conscious attitude of the authorities to deceive the peoples of another state and the cynical manipulation of public sentiment through the media are key characteristics of political processes at the global level.

Work on image creation is carried out purposefully and by various means on each of the channels of perception: visual, verbal, event and contextual:

- visual dimension forms the external image: compliance with the norms of business and official clothes, accessories, hairstyle, manner of behaviour, facial expressions, gestures;
- in the verbal dimension - culture of communication: speech, public speeches, reports, interviews, articles, business correspondence, ability to conduct a conversation on the phone;
- event dimension is the normative and ethical side of an act, behaviour, activity in general, i.e. we are talking about a person's reputation: the dynamics of image formation is determined by the subject's reputation;
- The contextual dimension is considered as joining the images of other people (relatives, friends, environment), which also influences the reputation of a person and the image as a whole. Therefore, in the work on personal image formation, the issue of reputation requires special attention.

The image of a leader is formed as a result of communication between the politician and the audience. In this regard, there are two important properties of political leadership:

- The leader for the public acts as a constructed image and therefore can have almost any given characteristics.
- For a leader, the questions of what personality traits determine his/her desire to become a leader become significant. The traditional problems of leadership psychology recede into the background:

identification of personality and character traits, the type of personality required in a particular situation.

There are various ways to manipulate information:

- distortion of information ranges from outright lies to partial distortions, such as falsification of facts or shifting the semantic field of a concept, when, say, the struggle for the rights of a minority is presented as a struggle against the interests of the majority;
- concealment one of the key groups of methods related to the construction of the leader's image at the municipal level in direct communication with the masses, i.e. there should be direct and feedback communication with the population. The way in which information is presented often plays a decisive role in ensuring that the content communicated is perceived in the manner required by the sender. For example, an abundance of raw and/or unsystematised information "can fill the airwaves with streams of worthless information, further complicating an individual's already hopeless search for meaning". Likewise, information presented in small portions does not allow it to be used effectively. In both cases, however, the reproach of concealing certain information is removed in advance.

In this regard, manipulation of information can lead to activity or passivity depending on what the manipulator needs. Thus, an image can be either active or passive.

Activity in one form or another manifests itself through appropriate behaviour, activity. There is no activity outside of activity, but not all activity is activity. However, it is active activity that allows to achieve goals in a shorter time, to identify and eliminate existing shortcomings in time, to solve problem situations. At the same time, excessive activity is fraught with conflicts, open confrontation, physical violence, etc.

Passive image can be characterised by the absence of feedback, i.e. as manipulative management. Such methods of management of the heads of power structures, the attitude to a person as a means of satisfying their own interests not only disorganise the socially active part of the population, cause psycho-emotional and social disorganisation, but also disorganise the socially active part of the population.

tensions, but also nullify the institution of social control as evidence of social activity of the population, its direct participation in state and municipal governance and civil control over them.

Manipulation manifests itself as an impact on the crowd, where the effect of financial incentives plays a major role, i.e. abstraction from theoretical cognition through the introduction of certain attitudes. To achieve control over the crowd, the effect of psychological contamination is used as a method of emotional generalisation of people, thus, to attract the attention of the masses, to cause their lively support, there is no need to appeal to everyone, it is more effective to establish verbal - non-verbal contact with the sociocritical core, to cause it to have an appropriate attitude to themselves.

§4.4 Digital diplomacy, means of rapid introduction of myths and values into mass consciousness

Public diplomacy is objectively becoming one of the main instruments of the global socio-political palette. Its skilful implementation together with the competent use of other "humanitarian resources" sometimes gives a state much more than it can claim by objective indicators of its political, economic and military power.

Researchers of public diplomacy in this regard emphasise: "The policy of forming a positive image of the state is implemented through information, political, diplomatic, cultural, power, economic and other actions of the state and its partners - public organisations, associations and individual citizens of the country. These actions are combined into information campaigns (operations), psychological operations of strategic, operational and tactical levels.

Mass media (mass media) - publicity, i.e. unlimited and over personal circle of consumers; availability of special, technical devices, equipment; indirect, separated in space and time interaction of communication partners; one-direction of interaction from communicator to recipient, impossibility to change their roles; non-permanent, dispersive nature of their audience, which is formed from case to case as a result of general attention shown to this or that programme or article.

The media not only criticise shortcomings in politics and society, but also fulfil the constructive function of articulating various public interests, constituting and integrating political actors. They provide representatives of various social groups with the opportunity to publicly express their opinions, find and unite like-minded people, unite them through common goals and beliefs, and clearly articulate and represent their interests in public opinion.

The functions of the media directly or indirectly serve the mobilisation function. It is expressed in inducing people to certain political actions (or conscious inaction), in their involvement in politics. The media have great opportunities to influence people's minds and feelings, their way of thinking, methods and criteria of evaluation, style and specific motivation of political behaviour.

In democratic states, the rational model of mass communications, designed to persuade people by means of information and arguments constructed in accordance with the laws of logic, clearly prevails. This model corresponds to the mentality and political culture of the people there. It offers competition between different media outlets for the attention and trust of the audience. In these states, the use of the media to incite racial, national, class and religious hatred and hostility is prohibited by law, but even in these states, various political forces widely use methods of predominantly emotional influence to propagate their ideas and values, which is especially evident during election campaigns.

The living word and visual image have a great power of emotional influence on the personality, which can often overshadow rational arguments and arguments. This is widely used by totalitarian, authoritarian and especially ethnographic regimes, abundantly saturating their political propaganda with emotional content that suppresses human reason. Here, the media widely use psychological suggestion methods based on fear and faith to incite fanaticism, distrust or hatred towards political opponents, persons of other nationalities and all undesirable people.

One of the most important means of political influence of the media is to identify topics and areas of discussion that focus the attention of the public and the government. The media usually determine for themselves what should and should not be put before the public. The choice of political topics and demands is made not only according to the predilections and interests of media owners and managers, but also under the influence of specific rules that emerge under the conditions of information pluralism in a modern market society. In this society, the main criterion of media success and the condition for the survival of most of them is the attention of the public. In order to attract this attention, the mass media, sometimes without even realising it, are usually guided by the following general principles when choosing topics for publications and programmes:

1. Priority, importance (real and imaginary) and attractiveness of the

topic for citizens. In accordance with this principle, the most frequent media reports deal with such issues as, for example, threats to peace and security of citizens, terrorism, environmental and other disasters, etc.

2. Uncommonness of facts. This means that information about extreme events - famine, wars, unusually violent crimes, etc. - dominates over the coverage of everyday life. This explains, in particular, the media's tendency towards negative information and sensationalism.

3. Novelty of facts. Reports that are not yet widely known can attract the attention of the population to a greater extent. It can be the latest data on the results of economic development or the number of unemployed, on the flight to other planets, on new political parties and their leaders, etc.

4. Political success. According to this principle, programmes and articles include reports on the successes of political leaders, parties or entire states. Special attention is paid to the winners of elections or rating polls. The cult of stars in politics, art and sports is a typical phenomenon for the media in a market society.

5. High public status. The higher the status of the source of information, the more significant an interview or TV programme is considered to be, since it is assumed that their popularity, all other things being equal, is directly proportional to the social status of the people reporting the information. By virtue of this rule, the persons who have the easiest access to the media are those who occupy the highest positions in the political, military, church or other hierarchies: presidents, military leaders, ministers, etc. They are devoted to the front pages of newspapers and headlines. The front pages of newspapers and the main radio and television programmes are devoted to them.

The greatest danger for citizens and the democratic state system is the use of SMI for political manipulation - the hidden management of political consciousness and behaviour of people in order to force them to act (or not to act) against their own interests. Manipulation is based on lies and deception. Moreover, it is not a "lie for salvation", but self-serving actions. Without a proper fight against manipulation, it can become the main function of the media and nullify the democratic principles officially proclaimed by the state.

Requiring greater flexibility in politics, manipulation as a method of

social management has a number of advantages for its subjects in comparison with forceful and economic methods of domination. It is carried out invisibly for the governed, does not entail direct sacrifices and bloodshed, and does not require large material expenditures, which are necessary to bribe or appease numerous political opponents.
The Global Information Network (Internet) is increasingly being used by participants in armed conflicts and geopolitical confrontation. As a communication channel, it provides a wide range of opportunities to influence public opinion, as well as political and economic decision-making.
The concept of "soft power" is increasingly used, which means a set of tools and methods of achieving foreign policy goals without the use of weapons - through information and other non-military levers of influence. All these methods are often used to provoke extremist speeches, manipulate public consciousness, and interfere in the internal politics of sovereign states.
US Army Information Operations Doctrine FM 3-13 describes tactics for offensive and defensive operations in foreign territories.
According to the US Department of Defense Directive DODD 3600, the Pentagon is giving priority funding to programmes to create automated battle management systems (ABCS), communications, intelligence, information and navigation systems directly for combatants, the prototypes of which have been tested during military operations in the Balkans, Iraq and Libya.
A special place in the "promotion of democracy" through "colour revolutions" is occupied by the formally independent governmental U.S. Agency for International Development (USAID), whose activities are focused on the "spread of democracy" and "consolidation of democratic regimes in the world". In addition to USAID, there are many non-governmental organisations (NGOs) that accumulate huge funds allocated by Congress and the US State Department to create outposts of American influence in foreign countries.
Such NGOs include, among others, the National Democratic Institute, the International Republican Institute, the International Foundation for Electoral Systems, the Open Society Institute, Freedom House, and the George Soros Foundation. It is through such organisations that coups are financed with the help of an extensive network of corruption, including businessmen, government officials, and the "alternative" journalistic corps.

There are several expressions used to refer to the way in which ICTs influence foreign societies: digital diplomacy, Internet diplomacy, eDiplomacy, digital media dip lomacy, social media diplomacy, Twitter diplomacy or Twiplomacy, public diplomacy Web 2.0. (Web 2.0. public diplomacy, cyberparadiplomacy and others.

Interaction in social networks can be divided into three levels: "technological" (issues of development of social platforms themselves), "civic" (involvement and participation of people in social networks) and "political" (use of technologies and environment to influence participants in digital interaction). Social networks are increasingly becoming a target for the dissemination of political information. Their main feature is that dialogue is the key form of contact with the audience, with the possibility of almost instant feedback.

One of the most important features of digital diplomacy is the ability to directly influence events and people in foreign countries, bypassing media filters and often even being outside the boundaries of sovereign and international law. This allows us to set our own rules of the game, seriously change the information picture and set the agenda.

§4.5 Improving inter-state relations on professional social networking sites

Today, there are seven driving factors that have the greatest impact on shaping the world situation and the emergence of new interstate conflicts. Among them:

- Demographic change, which means that by 2017 the world's population will grow by another billion people, and this will contribute to increased stability in some countries, while in others it will rock the situation and create new conflicts;
- The state of natural resources and the natural environment - first of all, the problem of food production and drinking water availability in the context of the growing needs of the world's population remains unsolved and particularly acute;
- Scientific and technological development, information technology can significantly alter the cycle of production and distribution on a scale that can be equated to that of the Industrial Revolution;
- The global economy and further globalisation of world production and the world market may lead to an inordinately high level of interdependence of countries, in which the threat of general destabilisation through a certain participant in the system and the chances of general

stabilisation under the influence of developed stable countries increase significantly;

- Governance structures within individual countries and on a larger scale, in which the role of national governments is retained, without taking into account that there are fewer functions in the areas of information management, technology transfer, disease control, control of population migration;
- Future conflicts, among which conflicts generated by three types of reasons remain particularly important: the desire to exploit the vulnerabilities of a country, in particular the United States, to weaken its international position in the event of involvement in an asymmetric conflict; the persistence of the threat of conflict involving weapons of mass destruction; regional contradictions; etc.

The basis of interstate conflicts is international relations. International relations are a set of economic, political, legal, ideological, diplomatic, military, cultural and other ties and relationships between entities operating on the world stage.

From the point of view of the theory of international relations interstate conflict is a type of international relations, the subjects of interstate conflicts are coalitions of states, individual states, as well as parties, organisations and movements struggling to prevent, end and solve various types of conflicts related to the administration of power functions. In accordance with this, define such types of interstate conflicts:

- Directly interstate conflicts (both sides are states);
- Wars of national liberation (one side is the state), anti-colonial, wars of nations, against racism, against governments;
- Internal internationalised conflicts (a state is an associate of one of the parties on the territory of another state).

The foundations of G. Morgenthau's theory of political realism are reduced to six principles (fundamental statements) from which all others are evident. These include:

- The principle of dependence of real phenomena and processes in the sphere of politics, as well as society as a whole, on objective laws deeply rooted in human nature has not changed since ancient times. It is expedient to improve society and act in the international environment only by understanding its laws, which cannot be interpreted at one's own discretion, as their action does not depend on the will of man;

- The principle of identification of interest and force, and in international politics - forceful harmonisation of interests between states. Power is necessary for a state for self-preservation (i.e. maintaining power on its own territory), but its accumulation leads to the establishment of power over other states and peoples;
- The principle of instability of interest and its changeability depending on circumstances and specific situation. Power, just like interest, depends on the environment and can encompass both physical violence and cultural influence, which allows controlling the behaviour of other states;
- The principle of inapplicability of morality in its abstract understanding to the actions of states in international relations. The criterion of foreign policy and morality in it is the result, which is measured by political consequences;
- The principle of non-identity of the morality of an individual nation with universal moral laws, where the government's policies are based on respect for the interests of other nations, it protects and realises the interests of its nation and demonstrates moderation;
- The principle of autonomy of foreign policy, as well as politics in general, from all spheres of international relations. Political realism recognises the importance of any spheres of social activity, but views them through the prism of politics and the needs and interests in the process of its implementation.

Researchers of the influence of mass media on electoral behaviour distinguish three models of voters' response to the impact of mass media:

1. A model of maximum information sensitivity in which the electoral preferences of audiences of a particular media outlet are directly related to the corresponding representation of a political party or politician in that media outlet.
2. A model of minimal information sensitivity, where there is no or no significant relationship between voter preferences and media information.
3. Inverse sensitivity model, i.e. the reaction of the audience of a particular media outlet is the inverse of the politician's presentation in that media outlet.

Analysing the information circulating in mass communication media also provides other opportunities. For example, consideration of various statements of a public figure in terms of the degree of flexibility or rigidity of his position allows us to determine the "space" left for political manoeuvre. Comparison of data on the balance of power in the political space under study can be the basis for inferences about whether the politician has real resources. In other words, it gives an opportunity to answer the classic questions of political science: who is, who is with whom, who is behind whom.

CONCLUSIONS TO CHAPTER IV

In this chapter:

- methods of creating virtual communicative information spaces of interstate relations are given;
- A schematic representation of the information and communication interaction process;
- The formation of communicative information strategies for regulating interstate relations is considered;
- methods and means of constructing the image of informants and their organisational structures are given;
- digital diplomacy as a means of operational introduction into mass consciousness is substantiated;
- systemic approaches to improving interstate relations on the platforms of professional social networks are proposed.

CONCLUSION

The problem of information security of economic objects is multidimensional and needs further elaboration.

In the modern world, informatisation is becoming a strategic national resource, one of the main assets of an economically developed state. The rapid improvement of informatisation in Uzbekistan, its penetration into all spheres of vital interests of an individual, society and the state has entailed, in addition to undoubted advantages, the emergence of a number of significant problems. One of them is the need to protect information. Given that at present the economic potential is increasingly determined by the level of information infrastructure development, the potential vulnerability of the economy to information impacts is growing proportionally.

Realisation of information security threats consists in violation of confidentiality, integrity and availability of information. From the point of view of the system approach to information protection, it is necessary to use the entire arsenal of available means of protection in all structural elements of the economic object and at all stages of the technological cycle of information processing. Methods and means of protection should reliably block possible ways of unauthorised access to protected secrets. Efficiency of information security means that the cost of its implementation should not be greater than possible losses from the realisation of information threats. Information security planning is carried out by means of development of detailed information protection plans by each service. There is a need for clarity in the exercise of powers and rights of users to access certain types of information, in ensuring the control of protection means and immediate response to their failure.

The research motivation of the author of this monograph is connected with the desire not only to study the problems of legal support for the development of the information society, which have not yet found an optimal solution and require the application of modern approaches.

At the same time, it should be noted that the theoretical issues of creating an information society and legal support of national information security have not been sufficiently researched. Determination of the directions of legal provision of national information security requires a systematic approach and legal assessments, taking into account the elaboration on the basis of analysis of the peculiarities of information relations related to the provision of national information security, the impact of globalisation processes on them.

The multifaceted nature of information relations and the need to regulate them require the development of a codified legislative act, as well as a draft framework for ensuring national information security.

LITERATURE USED

1. Popov V.D. Informatsiologiya i informatsionnaya politika. - M.: RAGS, 2005. - 120 c.
2. Voronov, K. V. Global intersystem: Evolution, structure, prospects / K. V. Voronov // World Economy and International Relations. - 2007. -№ 1. - C. 18-19.
3. Busygina, I. M. Political Regionology / I. M. Busygina - M., 2006.
4. Akhmetyanova A.I., Kuznetsova A.R. PROBLEMS OF PROVIDING INFORMATION SECURITY IN RUSSIA AND HER REGIONS // Fundamental Research. - 2016. - № 8-1. - C. 82-86;
5. Andreev O.O. Critically important objects and cyberterrorism. Part 1: System Approach to Organisation of Counteraction [edited by V.A. Vasenin]. - M.: MCNM, 2008. - 398 c.
6. Babash, A.V. Information security (+ CD-ROM) / A.V. Babash, E.K. Baranova, Y.N. Melnikov. - Moscow: Knorus, 2013. - 136 c.
7. Security of Russia. Legal, socio-economic and scientific-technical aspects. Fundamentals of information-psychological security: monograph. - Moscow: International Humanitarian Foundation "Znanie", 2014. - 416 c.
8. Vasilkov, A.V. Security and access control in information systems / A.V. Vasilkov, I.A. Vasilkov. - Moscow: Forum, 2015. - 368 c.
9. Gafner, V. V. Information security / V.V. Gafner. Gafner. - Moscow: Phoenix, 2014. - 336 c.
10. Devyanin, P.N. Security analysis of access control and information flows in computer systems / P.N. Devyanin. - Moscow: Radio and Communications, 2013. - 176 c.
11. Information security of open systems. In 2 volumes. Volume 1. Threats, vulnerabilities, attacks and approaches to defence / S.V. Zapechnikov et al. - Moscow: Mashinostroenie, 2016. - 536 c.
12. Salaya, L.K. English for specialists in the field of information security / L.K. Salaya, A.K. Shilov, Y.A. Koroleva. - Moscow: Helios ARV, 2016. - 208 c.
13. Fedorov, A.V. Information security in the global political process / A.V. Fedorov. - Moscow: MGIMO-University, 2017. - 220 c.
14. Mukhtarov F.M. "Digital diplomacy - a determining factor in the formation of international relations". "Ta'ilim va ilmiy tadkikotlar samaradorligini oshirishda zamonaviy akhborot-communication tekhnologii larining urni" mavzusidagi Respublika ilmiy-amaliy anjumani materiallari tuplami. Muhammad al-Khorazmiy nomidagi

TATU ^arshi filiali. 2017 yil 5-6 may, 127-131 betlar.
15.Mukhtarov F.M., Shklyarovsky B.A.. "Prerequisites for ensuring the confidentiality of information resources in the electronic government", Collection of reports of the Republican Scientific and Technical Conference "The importance of information and communication technologies in the innovative development of real sectors of the economy" part 1 , Tashkent, 6-7 April 2017, TUIT, 23-25 pp.
16.Yakubov M.S., Mukhtarov F.M.. "Digital diplomacy - a priority factor in the formation of interstate relations", International Scientific and Practical Conference "Eurasian perspective: problems of sectoral complexes and their solutions", Moscow 18 June 2017. , Infinity Publishing House, 119-122 pp.
17.Mukhtarov F.M., Tashmukhamedova D.K. "Ensuring confidentiality of information resources in e-government", Fergha- na Scientific and Technical Journal, Fergha- na, 2018. 22-volume No.1, 216-218 pp.
18.Mukhtarov F.M. "Network-centric approach of ensuring national security of the state in social networks", "Modern modification in the national education: theoretical and practical science", Collection international scientific articles, Volume III, p. 14-19, Mosscow January 2018 y.
19.Mukhtarov F.M. "Significance of information resources in the formation of international relations", "Modern modification in the national education: theoretical and practical science", Collection international scientific articles, Volume III, p. 19-26, Mosscow, January 2018 y.
20.Mukhtarov F.M. "Information technologies as a priority factor in the formation of the strategy of interstate vennykh relations", "International conference on importance ofinformation-communication technologies ininnovative development of sectors of economy", Proceedings of the international scientific-practical and spiritual-educational conference dedicated to the 1235th anniversary of Muhammad al-Khwarizmi, p. 440-444, Tashkent, April 5 - 6, 2018 y.
21.Mukhtarov F.M. "Multistage processes of information resources formation", International Scientific and Technical Conference "Perspective information technologies", Collection of scientific papers, Samara 14-16 April 2018, pp. 306-315.

22.Mukhtarov F.M. "Information technology priority factor in the formation of the strategy of interstate relations", International Scientific and Technical Conference "Perspective information technologies", Collection of scientific papers, Samara 14-16 April 2018, pp. 315-319.

23.Mukhtarov F.M. "Conceptual approaches to improve the national legislation in the field of information security", Worldsocialscience, Scientific - practical journal №1, pp. 64-69, 2018 y..

24.Mukhtarov F.M. "Methods of protection of national security from external and internal information threats", Toshkent, TATU "Muhammad al-Khorazmiy avlodlari" ilmiy amaliy va ahborot tahliliy journal 2017 y. No. 2-son, 18-24 betlar.

25.Mukhtarov F.M. "Regulating the strategy of interstate relations on the basis of digital diplomacy" "Akhbo-rot - communication tekhnologiyalarining rivozhlanish istik bollari" mavzusidagi Respublika ilmiy-amaliy anjuman ma'uruzalari tuplami. Karshi sh., Muhammad al-Khorazmiy nomidagi TATU ^arshi filiali, 2018 yil 20-21 april 918-921 betlar.

26.Mukhtarov F.M. "Algorithms for regulating the strategy of interstate relations on the basis of digital diplomacy" "Informatika, akhborot tekhnologiyalari va boshkaruv tizi-mi: bugun va kelajakda" mavzusidagi Respublika ilmiy-amaliy conference materialari tuplami 2-kism, Navoi sh., Navoi davlat pedagogika instituti, 2018 yil 20 April 118-122 betlar.

27.Mukhtarov Farrukh Muhammadovich "A conceptual model of information security in international relations" International Conference "Scientific research of the SCO countries: synergy and integration" April 26, 2018. Minzu University of China, Beijing, PRCp.145-151.

28.Mukhtarov F.M. "Methods of realisation of information resources in information society", "Infocommunications: Networks - Technologies - Solutions" scientific and technical journal, Tashkent 2018. 45-volume No. 1, pp. 55-61.

29.Mukhtarov F.M. "Ensuring information security of state secrets in the information environment" Bulletin of Tashkent State Technical University No.1, Tashkent. 2018, pp. 40-45.

30.Mukhtarov F.M. "Selection of priority factors of the conceptual model of state information security" International journal of innovative technologiesinso- cialscience. 4(8)Volume 3, p. 89-94,

WarsawPoland, June 2018 y.
31.Mukhtarov F.M. The selection of priority factors of the conceptual model of the state of information security// IJARSET: International Journal of Advanced Research in Science, Engineering and Technology. Volume: 05 Issue: 06 June-2018, India (#05) Global Impact Factor, IF=4.346.
32.Mukhtarov F.M. "Davlat boshkaruv idoralari ahborot resurslarari confidentialalligini ta'minlashning hukukiy asoslarari", Fargona sh., FarPi ilmiy-tehnika journal, 2018 yil 24-volume No. 3-son 216-218 betlar.
33.Mukhtarov F.M. "Basic principles of ensuring national information security", Fargona sh., FarPI ilmiy -tehnika journala, 2018 yil 24-volume #3-son 216218 betlar.
34."Akhborot havfsizligiga tahdidlar" - Idoraviy Journal 2011 yil.
35."Information security audit of a computer network" - Departmental Journal 2012.
36."Uzbekistan Respublika Respublika Respublika Respublika Respublika Respublika Republica" - Idoraviy Journal 2014.
37."Information warfare" - Departmental Journal. 2015.
38."Akhborot havfsizligini ta'minlashning siyosiy masalalalari" - Idoravi Journal. 2016 yil.
39."Akhborot havfsizligini ta'minlash - akhborot asreening dolzarb mu'ammosi" - Idoravi Journal. 2016 yil.
40."E-postada ahborotlarga nisbatan mavjud havf- khatarlarlar va ulardan ^imoyalanish asoslari" - Idoraviy Journal. 2017 yil.
41."On employee actions leading to improper possession of confidential information" - Departmental Journal. 2018 г.
42."Ensuring the confidentiality of e-government information resources"- Departmental Journal. 2018 г.
43.Krivoukhov A.A. Information security as a measure to ensure national security of Russia // State and Society: yesterday, today, tomorrow. Series: Law. 2013. №9 (3). C. 105-112.
44.Markov A. Processes of formation of information security of society. - Moscow: LAP Lambert Academic Publishing, 2011. - 532 c.
45.Arsenyan A.Z. National and international security: concept, peculiarities, legal bases of ensuring // Jurisprudence. - M.; Izd-vo RGGU, 2003. - № 3. - c.7-17.

APPENDICES.

Annex 1

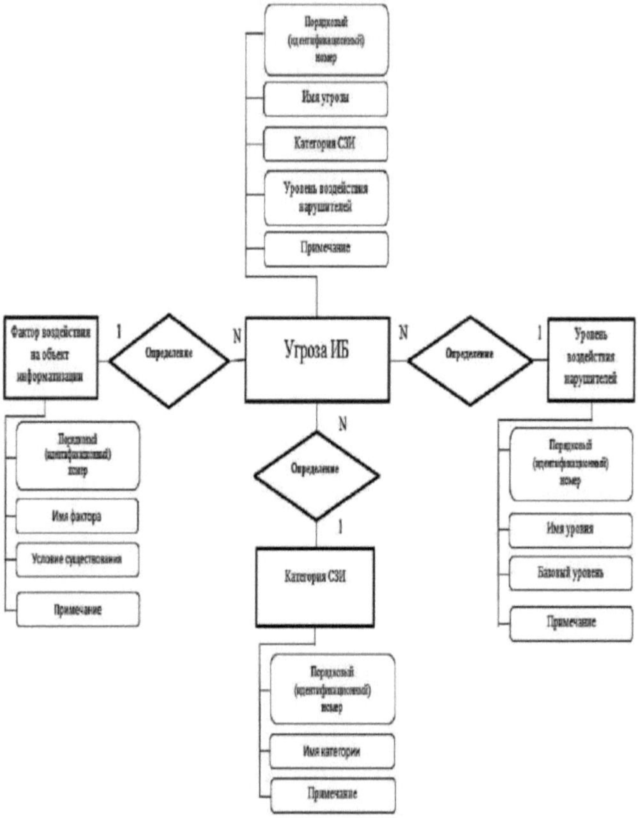

ER model of threat model database in Chen's notation.

Annex 2

Information Security Goals and Threats.

Annex 3

All threat sources can be categorised into classes based on the type of carrier, with classes divided into groups based on location.

Structure of the classification "Sources of Threats"

Annex 4

Vulnerabilities can also be categorised into classes based on the source of the vulnerability, classes based on groups and sub-groups based on manifestations.

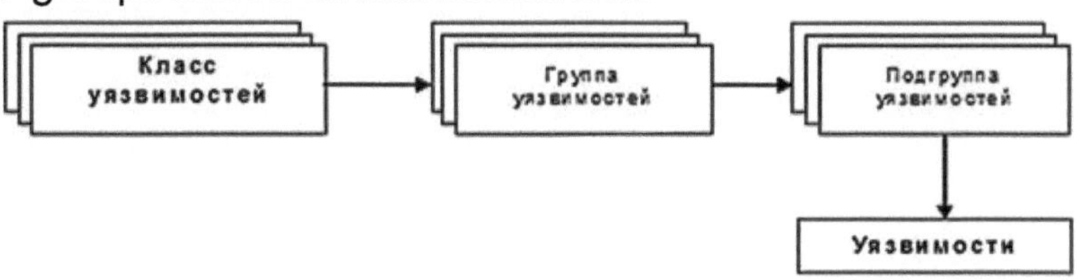

Vulnerabilities classification structure

Annex 5

Implementation methods can be divided into groups according to the way they are implemented.

Structure of the classification "Implementation methods"

MIX
Papier aus verantwortungsvollen Quellen
Paper from responsible sources
FSC® C105338

Printed by Books on Demand GmbH, Norderstedt / Germany